Prudish Nation

Paul Dalgarno

Paul Dalgarno is an author and journalist. He was deputy editor of The Conversation (Australia) and a senior writer and features editor at the Herald newspaper group (UK).

His other books are *And You May Find Yourself* (Sleepers, 2015), *Poly* (Ventura, 2020) and *A Country of Eternal Light* (Fourth Estate, 2023).

Paul Dalgarno

Prudish Nation

Life, love and libido

UPSWELL

First published in Australia in 2023
by Upswell Publishing
Perth, Western Australia
upswellpublishing.com

Copyright © 2023 Paul Dalgarno

The moral right of the author has been asserted.

ISBN: 978-0-645-53692-8

A catalogue record for this
book is available from the
National Library of Australia

Cover design by Chil3, Fremantle
Typeset in Foundry Origin by Lasertype

Upswell Publishing is assisted by the State of Western Australia
through its funding program for arts and culture.

Department of
**Local Government, Sport
and Cultural Industries**
GOVERNMENT OF
WESTERN AUSTRALIA

For anyone who's ever felt like a weirdo, and anyone who hasn't.

Contents

Glossary

Allosexual: A person of any orientation who feels sexual attraction to other people.

Asexual/ace: A person who doesn't experience (or rarely experiences) sexual attraction to other people and/or doesn't (usually) desire sexual contact.

Bi+: A person who is sexually and/or emotionally attracted to more than one gender.

Cisgender or cis: A person whose gender identity matches the sex they were assigned at birth.

Heteronormativity/heteronormative: the concept and/or bias that heterosexuality is the preferred or normal/natural type of sexual orientation.

Mononormativity/mononormative: The concept and/or bias that monosexual and monogamous relationships are the preferred or normal/natural type of relationships.

Pansexual: A person who is attracted emotionally and/or physically to all genders.

Nonmonogamous: Having – or being open to having – more than one partner, or having one partner but having sex or intimate experiences with other people as well.

Polyamorous, poly, polyam: A person who has – or is open to having – more than one romantic relationship concurrently.

Pro-domme: Professional dominatrix. A woman who performs the act/art of domination for a fee, usually as part of BDSM roleplay.

1
The snapshot

Do you remember what you were doing on the evening of August 10, 2021? I'll jog your memory. It was a Tuesday. The average temperature across Australia was 14 degrees Celsius. You were wearing ... hmmm ... what were you wearing? What did you have, or crave, for dinner? What about all the chatter in your mind, the victories, slights and snubs of the day – do you remember those?

I'm going to guess you either thought about, or made a concerted effort not to think about, Covid. If you were in Cairns or much of New South Wales, you were in lockdown. In Western Australia, Tasmania, ACT, the Northern Territory and South Australia, you probably thought at least once about your borders tightening while illness swept the landscape like clouds on the BOM radar, missing you, coming soon, just passed. Which isn't to say you were on your knees praying to your gods necessarily – you might have been watching TV, texting friends, doom-scrolling, happy-scrolling, stroking a pet, maybe even stroking yourself or a loved one – why not?

If you were in Victoria – as I was – you were five days into your sixth major lockdown, imposed fewer than ten days after the previous one ended. This so-called 'snap' affair stretched its arms into late October, dragging Melbourne through the sludge of 200 enforced home days to win the not-so-coveted title of Most Locked-down City on Earth.

If you had children of a certain age – as I did – they'd have been 'homeschooling', a euphemism that was becoming less and less fit for purpose. In my Year Five child's school assembly, which he attended from the landing outside his bedroom on a rickety desktop computer, the following tick-boxes were offered to assess the students' wellbeing:

☐   I'm great ☺

☐   I am okay

☐   I'm meh but I'll be okay

☐   I would like a check in!

I can't imagine the first box got much action in those dark and disorienting months.

Apart from matters of physical and mental health, you probably thought at least a couple of times that evening about relationships. With loved ones. Desired ones. Missed ones. Good-riddance ones. Lost ones. Never-were ones.

If you're otherwise struggling to recall what your life looked like on the evening of August 10, 2021, rest assured that the Australian Government has you covered – to a degree. As the largest statistical collection undertaken by the Australian Bureau of Statistics, the five-yearly Census collects data on the country's economic, social and cultural make-up, to inform policy and target resources. To make that sound less like bean-counting and more like human-being counting, the 2021 version came with a warm assurance that, beyond the raw data, 'every stat tells a story'. As Andrew Henderson, Census Executive Director and National Spokesperson said at the time: 'Every response matters, and yours does too. No community is too small to count. We want to make sure everyone is represented so we're urging people to complete now.'[1]

I needed little prompting – filling out online forms constituted a decent night's entertainment in those dreary days. My bigger concern was how to tell my story within the options provided. It wasn't going well.

I knew what my household looked like. My 12-year-old son was upstairs in his room with the door shut, despondent after a day of homeschooling in which he attended Google Meets with his camera off and told me to leave him alone any time I offered help, which was infrequently because I was downstairs in what had once been a lounge room attending Zoom meetings with the camera on for a job that would shortly end in redundancy thanks to the economic impact of the pandemic on the Australian university sector. My ten-year-old was in his dressing gown, which he'd not changed out of for days, moodily setting the table for dinner because it was his turn, a means of earning the pocket money he could theoretically spend at our local milk bar or somewhere else in our permitted five-kilometre radius. More often, he would trade the real-world cash for the digital V-Bucks he could spend on Fortnite, a far-fetched utopia where children, via their avatars, could congregate, play team sports and emote.

My partner, Kate, was serving soup and noodles into five bowls. She'd recently found employment again after the pandemic rendered the performing arts company she'd been working for redundant, in every sense. My wife, Jess, was on her phone, speaking to her mum – our children's grandma – who was at home 25 kilometres away in Donvale, which may as well have been Delhi given the travel restrictions. I was sitting at our kitchen table, nodding encouragingly at my younger son as he slapped down spoons, chop sticks and placemats, feeling annoyed that I couldn't even get past question-bloody-two in the census.

Who spent the night of Tuesday 10 August 2021 in this dwelling? Mark all that apply, like this: –

- ☐ You

- ☐ Spouse/partner

- ☐ Adult family members (including adult children, parents, siblings and extended family members)

- ☐ Babies, children and teenagers

- ☐ Unrelated housemates, flatmates or boarders

- ☐ Visitors or friends who will spend the night of Tuesday 10 August 2021 in this dwelling[2]

What I wanted to do, but couldn't, was amend the second box from Spouse-slash-partner to Spouse-plus-partner. Because that was my reality – the stat that would tell my story and theirs, the snapshot of my life and the lives of those I loved and lived with on Tuesday 10 August, 2021.

○○○

To be fair, I didn't need the ABS to remind me that my situation was unusual.

In 2020, I published a novel called *Poly* about a couple with young children who open their marriage and end up living polyamorously, which is to say: having, or being open to having, more than one romantic partner simultaneously, with the consent of everone involved. The topic interested me because it reflected my own life. My wife and I opened our marriage in 2016 and, like the characters in the book, found ourselves both together and seeing other people – a way of being that took us to new highs and lows of happiness, hangovers and heartache.

At the time of *Poly*'s publication, bookshops in Melbourne had been closed for many weeks and would remain so for many more. When they opened again, my novel was no longer – had it ever been? – on the New Release shelves. If I'd wanted to make sure nobody would ever see it, I couldn't have planned it better. But I'd made the decision months earlier, in agreement with my publisher, to be open about the fact I had IRL experience of polyamory. Why? I suppose I didn't want anyone to accuse me of writing about something I didn't know about, which – in matters of sex and sexuality – is fraught. That guy who made up a story about nonmonogamy without knowing the first thing about it? Not me, my friends. Here, look at my battle scars.

But it never sat well with me, that particular openness. Emma Viskic, the Australian crime writer, has no experience of being a private investigator, as far as I know, and yet her Caleb Zelic series reads as authentic and true.

The downside of my openness was this: for every question anyone asked about the novel during interviews and online book events, there were five or six about my personal life. I loved it whenever an interviewer asked about the novel I'd spent years writing. Less so the questions I couldn't answer readily and the rising terror of realising I was being positioned as a spokesperson for polyamory.

Let me be clear: I'm not a spokesperson for polyamory. Other people are, and they're far better at it – go speak to them or read their work. In the last couple of years, I've met plenty of polyamorous people who were sceptical about the way polyamory is portrayed in *Poly*, and quick to point out the characters are doing it 'wrong'. Clear communication, they've communicated clearly, is vital in poly relationships (my central characters, Sarah and Chris Flood, are bad at this); trust is critical (Sarah and Chris lie to themselves and each other); jealousy doesn't have to be destructive – it can be managed (Chris Flood, as befits his name, is frequently engulfed).

In tandem with this, it also dawned on me that I actually *was* a spokesperson, by default, and therefore had to tread carefully. Having come out as poly, it would seem weird to dismiss people's curious or well-meaning questions on the topic, however flat-footed, as if I was embarrassed or thought it was somehow shameful, which I don't. And so, I bumbled through answers as best as I could, to questions such as:

What is polyamory?

It's basically having more than one partner, or being open to that ...

And do the husband and wife have to agree?

Yeah, I guess. But it doesn't have to be a husband and wife, or a couple even. You can be single, a thruple, a quartet ...

Do you get jealous?

Me personally?

Yeah.

Yeah, I do, but the theory is you can get beyond that, to something called compersion, which basically means you're happy your partner is enjoying intimacy with someone else. I'm rubbish at it.

I'd get really jealous.

Right.

I don't think I could do polyamory.

Right, well ...

I just believe sex should be sacred – don't you?

Well, yeah, I ...

What's a normal day in the life of a polyamorous person?

Right, yeah, that's a tough one ... I'm guessing it would typically start with breakfast, maybe muesli or toast, a piece of fruit perhaps.

Is your narrator, Chris, gay?

Not particularly, no.

But he's polyamorous?

Yeah. You don't need to be gay to be poly, but you can be – it's up to you.

ooo

I wasn't the only one flummoxed by the 2021 Census. A non-binary option was included for the first time, augmenting the previous male/female either/or. But questions on sexuality and gender were notably absent, having been canvassed and then ditched. For gender, there was 'not sufficient confidence in the quality of the data that would be obtained'; while the draft sexual orientation questions raised 'sensitivities' such as 'privacy concerns, discomfort, or a lack of comprehension of the question'.[3]

Even though this left people feeling that they didn't count in an administrative process whose entire purpose was to count them, surely nobody was surprised. Bureaucracy always gets in the way – that's its superpower, which is why it's so easy to employ as a weapon, or shield, when expedient.

The Marriage Amendment (Definition and Religious Freedoms) Act 2017 followed a national postal vote to determine whether Australians *en masse* would consent to marriage between two 'people of marriageable age, regardless of their gender'. It was a big moment – one in which the wrecking balls of bias and bureaucracy stopped swinging long enough for people to gather their wounded and assess the damage that had been wrought. Wounds still smart on all sides of the debate but, some years later, the consensus must surely be that the world hasn't fallen apart – at least, not because Alice and Amy tied the knot. And why would it? Beyond John, James and their loved ones, who cares that he, she or they got married? What difference has it made to society more broadly? Not enough, some argue: the lightning rod of the marriage debate did what lightning rods do, drawing much of the energy crackling around LGBTQIA+ advocacy and running it deep underground.

Good thing it did, others might counter – we've been spared, if only just, a disaster of the sort best described in the 1984 film *Ghostbusters*:

> Fire and brimstone coming from the skies! Rivers and seas boiling! Human sacrifice, dogs and cats living together ... MASS HYSTERIA![4]

Too bombastic? During the same-sex marriage debate, Senator Cory Bernardi road-tested various slippery-slope arguments in a bid to illustrate how gay and lesbian marriages would upend Australia – views so lubricious that he himself would slide from his position as parliamentary secretary to former Prime Minister and fellow no-campaigner Tony Abbott in 2012.

A taste:

'There are even some creepy people out there ... [who] say it is okay to have consensual sexual relations between humans and animals. Will that be a future step? In the future will we say, These two creatures love each other and maybe they should be able to be joined in a union? I think that these things are the next step.'

And another:

'The next step, quite frankly, is having three people or four people that love each other being able to enter into a permanent union endorsed by society – or any other type of relationship.'[5]

The mechanics here are clear: take something supposedly cherished by your key demographic (marriage) and pose a threat by linking it to something the majority would presumably find objectionable (humans and iguanas getting it on).

And yes, as things stand, I'd likely vote against human–animal marriage, mainly for reasons of consent – although I do eat animals without their permission and wonder whether marriage to a human would be preferrable to starring in their stir-fry. If in the future there's a failsafe way to know a horse is champing at the bit to shack up with Kazza or Calum, I'd have to employ the same flow chart I use for all matters of consensual, age-appropriate relationships:

Is this purposely hurting anyone?

↓

No

↓

Is it any of my business?

↓

No

↓

Should I intervene?

↓

No

In Bernardi's second scenario, I can't see any problem with three or four people 'who love each other' being able to enter a union. Or rather, I can see *some* problems – mostly boring ones around red tape and the financial complications of multi-partner set-ups. But we already have lawyers charging $250 an email for the many marriages that break down in Australia, and the prospect of increasingly complex legal entanglements would surely have them salivating.

O O O

In writing this book, I've interviewed many people who are, or have been, in what might be considered unconventional relationships, or who have an unconventional identity, and the one thing in common is this: they're only unconventional in relation to an inherited assumption about what the world should look like – a view dictated in traditionally Anglo-Christian cultures by archaic interpretations of a group memoir written nearly two thousand years ago by men with conflicting accounts of the words and actions of another man who died decades before they started writing.

Clearly, then, books can and do have an influence. Most of the people I've spoken to are Australia-based authors who, in addition to living 'unconventionally', also write or speak publicly about sexual, gender or other distinctive relationship dynamics. I'll be honest up front and say that at no point did those conversations make me fear for the future of society. In some cases, I even felt hopeful – imagine! – that things are changing for the better; not that relationship types or identities within Australia are diversifying, but that we're becoming more willing to acknowledge, even fleetingly, how diverse we already are.

2
Hey prude

'Prudish' is never a compliment. It evokes a doily-straightening aunt, a vest-wearing uncle who finds pleasure only in god and garden. Prudes, by definition, are easily shocked by nudity and sex – although that would apply to all of us, surely, depending on the context. On a bus during rush hour, or during parliamentary Question Time ...

The real reason prudes get a bad rap, I suspect, has more to do with the evangelical overtones – and origins – of the word, the sense that prudes want to foist their self-righteous propriety on those they deem uncouth.

By the time of federation in 1901 Australia already had this type of prudishness baked into its bricks. Its uninvited settlers had persisted though a hellishly violent dispossessing era in which former convicts (mostly male) and later settlers and gold diggers (also mostly male) were tried in large numbers for 'unnatural crimes' (i.e. having sex with each other), the punishments for which included hanging. A renewed moral panic swept the country in the early 20th century, a period in which hetero sex was being touted more openly as a recreational and – whisper it – *fun* activity. Books such as the 1918 bestseller *Married Love* by British author Marie Stopes, promoted this idea, albeit still within the confines of a monogamous married couple. As explained in Frank Bongiorno's 2015 book *The Sex Lives of Australians*, *Married Love* and its ilk proclaimed that:

Sexual compatibility between a husband and wife formed the foundation of a successful marriage, with mutual orgasm the holy grail of every married couple – not, as medical opinion once held, because it was necessary for impregnation – but to preserve a happy and fulfilling relationship.[6]

The Customs Act and the Immigration Restriction Act – AKA the White Australia Policy – were the pegs that held down the tarp of Australia's federation in 1901. As the author Patrick Mullins points out when we speak, those founding documents were related in no small way to the moral tiz-woz in which the newly minted nation state found itself. The perceived need to project and protect what Australia *was* saw the government wrapping its clammy grip around everything from legislation to light reading.

Patrick's 2020 book *The Trials of Portnoy* casts a forensic eye on Australia's literary censorship regime – considered one of the harshest in the Western world for much of the 20th century – and the landmark court trails in the early 1970s following Penguin's publication of American author Philip Roth's masturbatory 1969 novel *Portnoy's Complaint*. Public interest in the trials was fuelled by a succession of high-profile witnesses speaking out in defence of the novel, including *Bobbin Up* author, Dorothy Hewett, who said:

'[The] value of [*Portnoy' Complaint*] seems to be, in fact, that it can teach Australians, notorious for their prudery, how to be honest about and with themselves.'[7]

Patrick is in Canberra, and we're chatting on Zoom, as I'll be doing for many, but not all, of the interviews thanks to Covid travel restrictions. We're watching each other in 2D as we build rapport via the NBN and discuss Australia's censorship and immigration policies.

'One of the first bits of legislation of the Federal parliament was the Customs Act of 1901,' he says. 'It essentially created the country by removing the borders between the colonies, making them state borders that were open for trade. I think that's a really important point.

'Modern, federated Australia was founded for trade reasons, for money. It wasn't really Parkes's "Crimson Thread of Kinship" that we often hear about.'

The 'crimson thread' – a term coined during a speech at a Federation Conference in Melbourne by New South Wales Premier Sir Henry Parkes in 1890 – referred to the shared Anglo–Celtic kinship of settler Australians, to the exclusion of all other nationalities and ethnicities, including – most pointedly – Indigenous Australians.

The rousing culmination of Parkes's speech – 'the time is coming when we shall all appear before the world as a United Australasia' – was reportedly met with self-assured cheers and confidently waving handkerchiefs by assembled politicians.[8]

But Patrick suggests the Customs Act a decade or so later – in addition to its financial motive – was born of deep anxiety.

'The Act also gave us the external border – "the continent for a country" idea – which we saw in defensive terms. As this far-flung enclave of white people, an island of the British Empire in the South Pacific, with a small population spread across the country, our governments thought that we were vulnerable – whether through foreign invasion or through new and radical political ideas.'

Censorship in the UK at the time was heartily exercised to counter advances in printing and the growing ease – and unease – with which people could disseminate information. Works that were seen as being misaligned with British values were banned, their authors demonised. This approach was adopted with gusto in pre- and post-federation Australia, with customs officers and police regularly going beyond the call of duty to stamp out radical or libidinous literature.

'Over time, the Australian authorities began to view themselves as being purer and more successful in this regard than Great Britain,' Patrick says. 'At one point, in the 1930s, there was talk of having a shared censorship treaty between Australia and the UK. We actually looked it over and thought, "Hmm, the British are a bit slacker on this than they should be".'

Policing morality went hand in (wringing) hand with anxieties about populating and building up the country. 'One way to do that was to promote a rigid set of cultural values and orthodoxies while trying to kill off anything that might threaten ideas around nation-building,' Patrick says. 'That meant the demonisation of homosexuality, of people having children out of wedlock, of divorce. No communism, socialism, realism – we didn't want that stuff.'

Realism of the sort espoused in the works of French authors Honoré Balzac and Émile Zola was particularly reviled, but those writers were hardly alone. The first half of the twentieth century saw an ever-expanding, and intentionally murky, list of banned books, covering everything from James Joyce to James Baldwin to James Bond. Innuendo of any kind was condemned but a special place in hell was reserved for what came to be regarded as sexually 'deviant' texts – which is to say, any and all that featured or obliquely hinted at extramarital sex, same-sex couplings or masturbation.

Even as the century wore on, stocking or circulating works by writers such as Hedy Lamarr and Jackie Collins would invoke heavy penalties and the very real risk of prison time for booksellers. Suitcases were ransacked at ports; raids were carried out on bookshops. Though the success of Penguin in the *Portnoy* trials signalled a step change, it wasn't definitive. Bret Easton Ellis's 1991 novel *American Psycho* was categorised under Australian censorship legislation as blasphemous, indecent and obscene, was banned outright in Queensland, and could only be sold elsewhere in a sealed plastic wrapper to over-18s – a proviso that continues today.

The climate of the censorship regime was stultifying for Australian authors not just because publication of anything even approaching the country's pre-approved moral boundaries was impossible for them but because much of the work being produced in the rest of the world was invisible. The late Western Australian author Peter Cowan, in a 1991 interview for the Battye Library collection, described Australia's literary censorship in this way:

> It had the effect of putting blinkers on the place for a great many years. But it wasn't as widespread [in the 1950s] as it was for instance in the 30s, when the very books you needed to know about, you had no way to know about them. At least you knew these books were there [in later years] – they were not available but you could try if you wanted to, to get them. We didn't even know what was not there in the 30s.[9]

As the 1970s progressed, the Censorial Eye of Sauron turned away from books and onto alternate and emerging means of disseminating 'harmful' views, such as magazines and TV, then videos and videogames – a change of tack that coincided with what Patrick wistfully refers to as the 'reduced cultural value' of books.

Does he think Australia is still prudish at heart? 'Yeah, definitely,' he says. 'I don't think that's changed and I don't think it's likely to change either. The prudishness of not wanting to talk about sex comes packaged with a whole lot of linked values that are conservative and which lead to further prudishness.

'The idea of home ownership is so strong in Australia, for example. But to buy a house nowadays, you generally need to have a relationship with somebody so you can have the dual earning power, and you need to have stable, well-paying jobs. You basically need to be somewhat conservative. You can't act like a revolutionary if you're going to get that security. And this continues to manifest in how we teach and react to change and diversity.'

I'm nodding because it sounds true but still, I can't help feeling surprised by Patrick's assessment, so ingrained is the stereotype of Australia as a fun-loving, if foundationally racist, country. 'The decision not to have landed gentry and titles in this country allowed us to develop this mythology of egalitarianism, with a culture that was going to be laid-back and relaxed,' Patrick says. 'But that's just not in tune with the reality.

'Australia is a middle-class, bourgeois country. We love rules and order. We don't want people to step out of line. We don't like queue jumpers, and we're constantly knocking on the bathroom door to find out what you're doing inside.'

○ ○ ○

There are no reliable and agreed-upon metrics for 'prudishness', of course, but I'm still keen to get people's views.

As the author Lee Kofman wisely puts it when I ask her on a warm Wednesday evening in Melbourne, it's all a matter of perspective, in her case informed by her life before arriving in the country more than 20 years ago. 'Having come here from Russia and Israel, I can definitely say it's less conservative in Australia,' she says.

I've known Lee since 2016, when I got in touch to tell her how much I'd enjoyed her 2014 memoir *The Dangerous Bride* – a book that considers nonmonogamy through various personal, cultural and philosophical lenses. I'm pretty sure I would have loved it whenever I'd read it, but I was especially besotted at that time because those were the very issues Jess and I were grappling with in our marriage. We wanted to stay together, we loved our family – but we also wanted to see other people. Was that weird? Was it possible? How would it work? Did anyone else do that kind of thing? Were we asking too much from life? *The Dangerous Bride* not only helped me get my thoughts in order but thrilled me as a piece of writing.

Since then, Lee and I have become firm friends. She launched my novel *Poly* in 2020 – over Zoom, of course – and I sang with my partner, Kate, at the launch of Lee's latest book, *The Writer Laid Bare: Emotional Honesty in a Writer's Art, Craft and Life.*

As Lee makes clear in *The Dangerous Bride*, nonmonogamy comes in as many shades as monogamy, with as many preferences, agreements and nuances as the number of individuals involved. Polyamory – in theory at least – puts a premium on communication and checking in with your partners' feelings, to what, for some, can seem like an excessive degree. Swinging, meanwhile, tends to refer to singles and/ or partnered people having no-strings sex with others. 'Don't ask, don't tell' is another type of nonmonogamy in which people know and consent to their partner(s) being nonmonogamous but don't necessarily want – or expect – to hear about their sexual activity.

Lee has a particular affinity with the last of these, and with it 'the mystery, the flirtatiousness, not knowing what's going to happen next. For me, it's about breaking the rules, about naughtiness.'

If that sounds transgressive, bear in mind that affairs occur in roughly 70 per cent of Australian marriages. By their nature, those affairs are secret (until they're not) whereas nonmonogamy of the sort Lee is discussing is an agreement between consenting partners.

'When it comes to relationships, we're actually quite prudish in Australia,' she says. 'Despite all the freedom around hook-ups, all the polyamory negotiations and discourse about queerness, there's a huge cultural emphasis on openness. And to some extent that's great. But I think we're taking it a bit far because it can stifle relationships in some ways. You can lose a little of the mystery.'

It's possible, she says, to walk the tightrope between the ethics of honesty (good) and the moral fervour (not so good) of our moment.

'I'm not saying people should cheat,' she says. 'I've been cheated on enough times in my life and I didn't like it, but we're in this therapeutic culture where there's a push to tell the truth at all costs rather than being diplomatic. Sometimes that comes from a very selfish drive to be unburdened, but you actually just end up burdening the other person instead.

'I think openness is great, just as I think monogamy and nonmonogamy are great. But, for me, nothing's great when it's compulsory. I mean, it's a cliché, I know, but if your girlfriend asks, 'Does my ass look big in this?' and you say 'yes' you'll get in trouble, won't you? Some things are OK to be left unsaid.'

○○○

At times, I can barely hear Christos Tsiolkas, author of books including *Damascus*, *The Slap* and most recently *Seven and a Half*, even though we're sitting a metre apart in his Melbourne studio.

The rain's coming down hard, there's thunder and lightning. But his frequent laughter cuts through everything, including when I ask if he thinks Australia is prudish. 'I used to think it was until I went to the UK,' he says. His laughter is infectious – and his point about the UK not lost on me.

I was born and raised in the north-east of Scotland and grew up in a nominally Episcopalian household, a branch of Protestantism that seasons its inherent uptightness with generous sprinklings of Anglicanism and Calvinism, as best summed up in joke form:

Why don't Calvinists have sex?

In case people think they're dancing.

So yes, the prudish UK, I know it well.

'I'm being a bit facetious,' Christos says. 'To answer you honestly, I do think there's a difference to notions of the body and sexuality between Western Europe, for example, and Southern and Eastern Europe. I remember being in Greece as a young man. A friend of my cousin's, a cis straight male, was hugging me and kissing me on the lips, and I thought, "Wow, that would not happen in Australia. That kind of physicality". It's not about romanticising the culture – it's just a different way of being in the body and being around others.'

Anglo Australia has inherited the UK's 'squeamishness around sex,' he says. 'You know, as a writer, I can't believe the English have a Bad Sex in Writing Award. It's so Benny Hill.' Again, the joyous laughter. 'You know, my parents love Benny Hill, and I actually love that smutty British humour too because it's really funny. It's delightfully camp. A lot of the problem for me at the moment in writing and art is that it's become really humourless.'

Given Christos's body of work has consistently featured gay characters, including, in his 2019 novel *Damascus*, homosexual Biblical characters, it's safe to assume he would have remained unpublished in any sort of traditional way during Australia's decades of harsh censorship.

OOO

The same goes for Peter Polites, who – like Christos – is an Australian of Greek descent. His 2019 novel *The Pillars* offers a deliciously satirical look at aspirationalism through Australia's working-class migrant communities and the booming Sydney property market. It also features gay meth-fuelled orgies.

I get the sense speaking to Peter that not writing and publishing those sex scenes would have felt more outrageous than doing so. As a gay man in Western Sydney, he wittingly and unwittingly pushes buttons.

'When I went to university, a lot of people were like, "Hey, let's do transgressive art",' he says. 'Their idea of that was rolling around on plastic bags. I was fucking embarrassed for them. I hold my partner's hand in Sydney's Western Suburbs and might get bashed, so don't talk about transgressive performances – you don't know shit.'

Like Patrick Mullins, Peter thinks Australia has sold itself on an 'all good, mate' attitude that's off-kilter with reality.

'I've had editors say to me, "Why do you keep on having sex scenes in your books?" And I'm like, "Read it properly. Those sex scenes are metaphors for war – that's why I use war-based language in them". I haven't had an editor say anything about the ritualised violence that appears in other people's writing but, oh, yes, my sex scenes are overdoing it.'

Of course, it's possible to make war *and* love, and to make readers hot and heavy while doing so. Peter readily admits he wants to turn people on with his sex writing.

'Prudish people have a deep loathing for their own bodies,' he says. 'I want gay men to read my sex scenes and be aroused. That's my goal. And a lot of lesbian and straight women love reading gay sex scenes too. I want them to love it. I want people's bodies to come alive when they're reading my books.'

In the case of *Poly*, I struggled to find ways to make the characters' bodies come alive while writing the sex scenes. If you've ever watched real-life, regular people having sex at close quarters, you'll know there's a world of difference between the physical and emotional immersion of being part of the action and sitting on the sidelines. Mainstream porn, I think, is a different kettle of fish – a pantomime version of sex that's heightened by exaggerated noises and actions. As I wrote on Lee Kofman's blog just after *Poly*'s release:

> There's a power dynamic in sex writing that reflects the dynamics we're likely to experience during sex, the big difference being that writing tends to be the work of a single mind – more masturbation than sex, with all the fantasy and wish-fulfilment self-pleasuring brings. And historically, that onanistic outpouring has overwhelmingly been the product of a straight male imagination.

This presented a challenge to me as a cis-het man while I was writing *Poly*, a novel about love and sex, with a straight male first-person narrator who has two female partners. #MeToo also happened while I was wrestling with this, a movement that highlighted more starkly than ever the prevalence of sexual abuse and gendered power imbalances.

So how, then, to write sex authentically, especially if we sympathise with psychotherapist and author Esther Perel's famous statement that 'we want between the sheets what we protest in the streets'?[10]

The answer, for me, was to be clear about the physical details, keep a sense humour without putting anyone down, and choose my metaphors carefully. Here's how that looked in practice:

Sarah curled into me, a dust storm of pheromones I knew I could survive, as always, by shallow-breathing. But then – a kiss on my shoulder, another on my upper arm. I turned onto my side to face her, stroked her hair, bunched it in my fist. Her fingers on my chest, teasing; taking my hand and guiding it between her legs. Her mouth finding mine, her kisses, the earth taste I'd missed and martyred myself for.

And then, shortly after:

She raised her hips to meet mine with every thrust while I did everything I could not to climax too soon. Eyes closed, I imagined Sarah without skin, my gran eating breakfast, my teeth being removed and replanted upside down – rooted.[11]

I can't help thinking, in speaking to Peter and reading his work, that his sex writing is more startlingly direct and embodied (but not without excellent metaphor and humour). Or does it just feel that way because it's between men and I'm less used to seeing that and less familiar with the power dynamics at play both in the depiction and lived experience of gay sex? In *The Pillars*, he writes:

The sex ranged from sensual to a series of athletic positions. I could have been in a pump'n'dump car wash or a blow'n'go Slurpee dispenser. My skin became numb to his touch and as a result my brain became deprogrammed to him as a person. Getting used to his body parts in me, getting used to his ideas being inserted into me.[12]

'Sex is just a conversation between two bodies and that shouldn't be stigmatised,' he says.

○ ○ ○

The Australian poet and novelist Omar Sakr's 2022 novel *Son of Sin* is a coming-of-age story about a queer Muslim boy called Jamal in Western Sydney. It's a beautiful novel, as much about culture, racism and religion as it is about sex, although sex – and particularly gay sex – is what's being referenced in the 'sin' of the title. Jamal sees it as the 'ultimate taboo' – a desire and activity that brings bliss and shame in equal and competing measure. Take Jamal's first sexual encounter, with Bilal:

> The sourness of [Bilal's] sweaty underwear. Jamal soaked it in saliva, lapping at the thick twitching dick, like he was still afraid to have nothing between him and his desire, needing even this thin layer of protection. And then he couldn't take it anymore, he released what was his, opening wide to suck on the brazen bald head. It was warm and hard and perfect in his mouth. He couldn't believe how it seemed to fill everything inside him.
>
> He was a faggot, oh God he was a fag, and he fucking loved it.[13]

If the particulars of the story come as a surprise it's because – as per the book's marketing – it's the first Australian novel by a queer Arab Muslim man, and each of those monikers – Australian, queer, Arab, Muslim, man – is interrogated individually and collectively.

For Omar, when we speak, Australia's prudishness is self-evident.

'Australia has a deeply repressed culture that is aggressively hostile to honest reflection, which requires vulnerability and trust,' he says. 'Both these qualities are in short supply in any imperialist colonial outpost – because such reflection could conceivably lead to a freer state of being.

'This is no doubt directly related to the fact that the majority of our media and politics is directed by old white men who make up 10 per cent of our population, but over 90 per cent of our government body and corporate CEOs.'

The policing effect of that heavily loaded media and societal bias is significant, he says. 'Lebanese masculinity is different to Australian masculinity in many ways. It's much more comfortable with sex, with dancing, with male intimacy.

'Growing up, I found myself watching in real time as the boys of my generation slowly lost all of what I saw evident in Arab men.

'Even among Western countries, from my experience, Australian prud-ishness, sexism, and homophobia is easily the worst. The straitjacket of Australian masculinity is wound so tight it's strangling everyone.'

Neither of us – nor Lee, Peter and Christos for that matter – would have had our work published in Australia's not-so-distant past. Had it somehow made it to print, it's probably safe to assume that Omar, Christos and Peter would come under immediate legal scrutiny, given homosexuality wasn't decriminalised until 1975 at the earliest in Australia (with South Australia the first juristriction to do so) and as recently as 1997 in Tasmania. Lee would most likely have been pilloried for non-judgementally discussing – and therefore promot-ing – extramarital sex, as would I. Without question, all of us would have manifestly failed to meet Australia's standards for normal and acceptable behaviour.

Which raises a number of questions, not least: what exactly is 'normal' when it comes to sex and relationships and who gets to decide?

3
Are you normal?

Ruth Dawkins and her husband, Young, are, in Ruth's words, 'the world's most boring couple'. Like many of us these days, they work from home, Ruth as a freelance writer, Young as a fundraising consultant and poet.

They hail from different parts of the world – Ruth from the Isle of Harris in Scotland, Young from the east coast of the US. They moved to Tasmania in 2013, a great fit, Ruth says, for their family. When Ruth and I speak, their son Tom is on the brink of adolescence. That Young gets mistaken for Tom's grandfather rather than his dad is sometimes embarrassing, occasionally annoying, and often a chance for Tom's classmates to show their support.

'We try to give Tom language to use in those situations, to just deal with it as quickly as possible,' Ruth says. 'A lot of the other pupils really like Young – they respond to his energy. He goes into their class and does performance poetry with them. When some other kid from school says something like "Is that your grandpa?", the kids from Tom's class step in and say, "Don't be rude – that's Tom's dad".'

Ruth was in her early twenties when they got together, Young in his late fifties. She was a student president at the University of Edinburgh, where Young was the Vice Principal, 35 years her senior. If by now you're thinking 'oh dear,' know that Ruth and Young were way ahead of you.

'We talked about all the reasons why it wasn't the best idea for us to be together,' Ruth says. 'The fact we had a professional relationship was as big a deal for us as the age gap. It was a bit … "scandalous" isn't the right word but, yes, it was absolutely scandalous. Especially somewhere like Edinburgh where they're all tweed suits and stiff upper lips.'

Of course, wanting to care for and invest in each other was a perfectly valid reason to continue. 'You reach the stage that everything is pointing towards this being a good thing,' Ruth says. 'If all that's holding you back is other people's judgement then it's definitely worth giving it a go.'

Tasmania, Ruth says, has a greater number of conspicuous age-gap relationships than any other place she's lived. Young is still older than most dads at the school pick-up but not by a huge margin.

'People don't spend a lot of their time down here being snarky about other people,' she says. 'Or maybe we just don't notice. We're so used to ourselves, so comfortable in our own identity as a family. Maybe we're leaving a trail of stink-eye behind us but are just not aware of it.'

A 2011 article Ruth wrote[14] for *The Guardian* titled 'He's not my father, he's my husband' gained considerable attention. For the Washington Post in 2018 Ruth wrote about how that initial piece had opened the floodgates to hundreds of letters and emails from people – almost always women – who were also in relationships with significant age gaps.[15]

'It's very strange,' she says. 'I find it quite surprising, the intimate details people will spill to a complete stranger. Because the *Washington Post* piece was syndicated internationally, I now get lots of emails in Spanish and Italian that I don't know how to even begin answering. It's touching and kind of sad that people are so desperate for advice that they'll email someone like me looking for it. I'm not an expert on any relationship, not even my own.'

Lots of the situations outlined in those emails, Ruth says, are 'crawling with red flags' – not because there's an age gap but because the relationships are being conducted in secret, almost always at the man's behest. 'The women don't seem too fussed about that bit, though,' Ruth says. 'Mostly they're thinking thirty years ahead, to what happens if the man becomes sick and they have to be his carer? What happens if he no longer wants sex or becomes sexually unattractive?'

Naturally, she says, the emails skew heavily to those with concerns and problems in their relationships – which is not to say there's such a thing as a trouble-free union.

In 2020, Young endured several months of treatment for cancer – a frightening time for the family. 'We were like "OK, this is us in the place we imagined we may end up when we talked about things 17 years ago",' she says. 'We've always known we're not going to get as long together as other couples, but I think going through that made Young's mortality feel very real to us in a way it hadn't been before.

We were literally talking about what was going to happen if and when he died, who was going to help with Tom, whether I was going to stay in this house or even stay in Tassie. But he had such determination to do everything within his power to have the cancer fuck off – the nurses said they'd never seen anyone come through his specific treatment the way he had and that his relationship and family had obviously helped him through.'

For me, mortality, the sad fact of it, is one of – maybe *the* – main reason I try to keep my nose out of other people's choices generally and romantic lives specifically. We will all either grieve or be grieved by those we love – or, in a worst-case scenario, by nobody. Is the person you love a man, a woman, a trans, nonbinary or genderqueer person, someone younger or older than you, lighter-skinned or darker, taller or shorter, hairier or smoother? Do they speak with an accent, have funny teeth, use a wheelchair, slurp their soup? Are they admired by their peers, misunderstood, depressed, repressed or elated? Maybe all that matters ultimately is that we find ways to care and be cared for while we can.

But still, we're a nosey bunch. 'In the early days, especially, we definitely got a lot of looks,' Ruth says. 'Probably because I was still dressing like a student and looked about fifteen. But that doesn't necessarily mean people have bad intentions – maybe they just wanted to know what the dynamic was. When we're out with new people these days, we make it clear to everyone we're married right away so we can get on with talking about more interesting things.'

Ruth and Young's age gap is of the sort we're all accustomed to seeing or hearing about – a younger woman with an older man and all the scuffed baggage that comes with. The woman *must* be a trophy wife, surely. He's *obviously* in it for the sex. She's *obviously* in it for the money. Even if the individuals in question *are* openly and unashamedly in it for those very reasons, it's hard to resist the negative pull of those judgements.

Older-man-younger-man relationships, while barely worthy of a raised eyebrow in Ancient Greece, say, can make eyebrows nearly come off these days, depending on the couple. Stephen Fry's engagement to his now-husband, Elliot Spencer, thirty years his junior, launched a thousand snippy op-eds in the mid-2010s that could basically be boiled down to: a British national treasure is breaking an unspoken taboo right in front of our faces and we feel really, really strange about it. Headlines about older-woman-younger-woman relationships range from the incredulous to the prurient, whereas older-woman-younger-man media narratives work hard to conjure a sense of disbelief.

Try reading anything about Jada Pinkett Smith without being prompted to believe, with varying degrees of subtlety, that her supposed 'entanglement' with singer August Alsina was shocking for two reasons: she was married to actor Will Smith at the time and she was 21 years Alsina's senior. If we know the late fashion designer Dame Vivienne Westwood was 25 years older than her husband Andreas

Kronthaler, it's because it was – and still is – mentioned any time they are. Likewise the 32-year age gap between American actors Sarah Paulson and Holland Taylor.

Is this, as a *Psychology Today* article put it in 2021, a prejudice informed by the belief that the older person 'is reaping more rewards from the relationship than the other person'?[16]

And if so, does the size of the gap matter? Apparently, yes.

As Deakin University's Associate Professor Gery Karantzas writes in the overview for the university's Mind the Gap project:

> Studies have found partners with more than a ten-year gap in age experience social disapproval. But when it comes to our own relationships, both men and women [...] are open to someone 10–15 years their junior or senior.'[17]

Still, being open to something isn't the same as signing up for it.

Back in 2013, in its last published Social Trends report, the Australian Bureau of Statistics found that only 8 per cent of opposite-sex couples had an age gap of ten years or more, with an average gap of just 3.7 years. For women in same-sex couples, those with a decade-or-more age gap rose to 15 per cent (with an average gap of 4.8 years); while some 25 per cent of men in same-sex relationships had an age gap of ten-plus years, with an average gap of 6.5.[18]

In 2018, meanwhile, the ABC reported that only about 1% of opposite-sex age-gap couples involve an older woman with a younger man,[19] perhaps explaining why those pairings exert a particular hold on tabloid journalists the world over.

○ ○ ○

I meet author and editor Angela Meyer at a café on a sunny day in Melbourne's Elsternwick. I'm a big fan of Angela's 2018 novel *A Superior Spectre*, which I've brought in the hope she'll sign it. A genre-bending story, it features a dying man, Jeff, in a dystopian present who, via experimental technology, enters the mind of an unwitting nineteenth-century Scottish woman, Leonora, feeling conflicted, as he always has, about the way he is:

> You see I wouldn't want you to think that my shameful desires precluded me from being attracted to women, from loving a woman. There still seems to be a deep misunderstanding, in my experience, about how complex sexuality can be, and about our capacity to desire so much, so many different types of people, at once.[20]

We're going to be talking about bisexuality and shame – how they intertwine in the novel and in Angela's life. And we'll get to that later in the book, but for now we're talking age gaps.

'My partner, Christopher, is 12 years younger than me so that's a bit unconventional,' Angela says. 'I mean, we've definitely encountered people who see it that way.

'At first, his parents were a bit wary. I understood that, because he was only twenty when we met – he was just coming into the world and figuring out who he was. But we just knew immediately how strong our connection was, and for me it's the most mature relationship I've ever had. We were kind to each other, we'd listen to each other, we had fun together – it was an adult relationship.'

Lots of the people I've spoken to for this book have witnessed a particular type of reckoning that fascinates me – one that forces their loved ones to reconcile a stereotype (what a gay person *is*, what a bi+ person *isn't*) with the living, breathing human in front of them. It doesn't always go well, or smoothly, but a bubble is still burst, an assumption – or fear –challenged.

'It didn't take long for Chris's family to get it, once they saw us hanging out together,' Angela says. 'They could see how silly we were together, all that stuff. His mum calls us "the lovebirds" now – it's really sweet.'

Five years on, Angela still picks up on shady aspersions from time to time, which are often hard to put a finger on. 'You just get the feeling from some people in your life that they think the age gap's a little ... unusual,' she says. 'Or sometimes that they see me as a bit predatory, you know – a cougar.'

She's long been looking for someone to build a family with, she says, yet certain people she cares for struggle with this notion. 'I've always wanted children,' she says. 'But some people presume, because I'm dating a younger man and have been in an open relationship, or because I'm bisexual ... I've actually had a few people say to me directly: "What – *you* want children?" It's as if all those other aspects of my so-called unconventional life have put me in a different category for them.'

Happily, since speaking with Angela in Elsternwick, she and Christopher have announced both their engagement and the birth of their first child.

○ ○ ○

It's uncontroversial to suggest relationships between sex workers and their clients are transactional – a service is provided and money changes hands. But it would be naïve to think of that transaction as cut and dry, or without emotion in the same way as, say, ordering groceries online. In a 2023 episode of The Ezra Klein Show podcast, the celebrated US relationship columnist and author Dan Savage said the following:

> I think all relationships, if you really peel the layers back far enough, are, at some point, transactional. I pay for it with my husband. I don't pay for it with cash money. I pay for it with time, attention,

affection, concern, making sure he goes to see the doctor when he needs to go see the doctor. There's a reason married people live longer. If I stopped paying in like that, if I stopped caring about him, if he stopped paying in like that, stopped paying me with those same ephemeral, intangible, but very important things, our relationship would collapse.[21]

Where there's an intimate or personal investment into giving and/or taking there is a relationship, whether it's momentary or lifelong.

I'm at a Brunswick café chatting to author Mia Walsch, whose 2020 memoir *Money for Something* focuses in large part on her occupation as a sex worker in Sydney's sex parlours and beyond. It's about Mia, but it's also about the people she worked with and got to know.

One of the most enjoyable – and refreshing – aspects of the book for me was that it never felt like a redemption story or morality tale. I loved it. Yes, Mia faces obstacles, struggles with mental health and smokes a prodigious amount of weed, but the solution for what ails her isn't renouncing sex work, an occupation for which she feels suited, and, on the whole, enjoys. As she writes:

> There are a few generalisations I would make about sex workers: they are all extremely interesting and complex people. Most of them are good people in their own various ways. They're strong and capable, working a job with not only a high emotional output/input, but also one that requires facing a great deal of stigma from all sides: the wider world, as well as those close to them.[22]

When we meet, it's been months since she stepped into the dungeon she works at as a professional dominatrix, or 'pro-domme', but that has everything to do with Covid-era restrictions and nothing to do with Mia's preferences.

'The relationships you have with your co-workers are always intense because you're in a super-intense environment,' she says. 'Working in a dungeon for six years created a little family for me, and I'm always looking for that, I guess, because I don't really have one. But that's not always a good thing because colleagues don't necessarily want to be your friends or family. I find that's a trap I fall into a lot.'

Boundaries blur elsewhere in the job too. 'Client–provider relationships are really interesting because they're all so different,' she says. 'Just like you have different relationships with friends. I have some clients who either end up being buddies or falling in love with me. Neither is great, really. For me, I find the idea of a client falling for me terrifying, so I always try to keep a separation between myself and my work.'

Mia's shoulders look relaxed whereas mine are at my ears. I'm scared of embarrassing her, or me, if any of the other people in the café hear me asking questions about sex work. Which – let's face it – is probably my inner prude coming to the fore.

'I've had some relationships with regular clients that were just lovely,' she says. 'We had a fun, sexy time and were able to leave it at the door. It's a relationship in the moment and when it's over, it's over. But you do build up feelings with regulars, depending on how often you see them and what activities you do. I have one client who I would see once a week and that became really intense, and yeah, I cared about him quite a lot.'

As a dominatrix, the care-giving aspect of Mia's work is multidimensional: there's the physical care and expertise needed to avoid injuring clients during role-play but also the emotional aftermath. 'When you stop doing the activities, you bring the client back into real life,' she says.

'There's something we call the "sub-drop", where a client can get really depressed. For the provider, there's also the "top-drop". You can feel down after dominating someone because of all the energy you've expended and how exhausting it can be mentally. It really takes it out of you.

'Aftercare can be different things, maybe cuddling or just chatting, or going through stuff that came up during the session – it just depends on what the person needs.'

I wonder if those intimacies – the cuddles, the talking through of shared experience – would be as hard, if not harder, to deal with than the sexual interaction for clients' partners, assuming they knew.

'A lot of the people you're seeing are married or in long-term relationships,' Mia says. 'That can be hard to deal with on your part, but also in terms of other people's judgement of you and the stigma. The truth is that sex workers are not trying to steal anyone's partners – I can guarantee you that.'

In practice, she thinks, they may actually be helping people's relationships, if only as a side-effect.

'Some sex workers are actually home-savers because they're giving somebody something they need that they obviously can't get elsewhere. It makes them more inclined to continue in their marriage or partnership, or with their family. The sad thing is, I reckon some of their partners would understand their needs and either be happy for them to see someone else or try to do that thing, whatever it is, themselves.

'I have one client who's always trying vanilla relationships but they don't work because he's obviously into what he's into. He'll stop seeing me for a while and then come back. It always makes me really sad because it's like: "You need this, but unfortunately can't find someone to give it to you so you're trying to squish down your desires and they'll always come bubbling up in the end".'

○○○

I first met writer and broadcaster Jinghua Qian on Zoom for a panel discussion we took part in with Lee Kofman at the Wollongong

Writers Festival in 2020, and much of what was said that day has stuck with me.

Jinghua – whose pronouns are 'ey' and 'eir' – has written and broadcast for Overland, Sydney Morning Herald, ABC TV, The Monthly and many other places. Whereas for me nonmonogamy has been explored as a breach of 'the norm' in adulthood, Jinghua has been nonmonogamous since ey was 15 and, as a nonbinary queer, comes from a different starting point.

'Part of what drew me to polyamory and nonmonogamy as a teenager was the resistance to defining things absolutely,' ey says the day we meet for coffee in Footscray. 'A resistance to saying a relationship that's romantic or sexual, or has a sexual component, is categorically different from every other kind of intimacy. As a teenager, you're having these really intense intimate friendships because you're going through adolescence together, and these are not necessarily the people you're having sexual interactions with.

'I went to an all-girls school, so that was clearly a gendered environment. I remember feeling discombobulated that no-one was on the same plane of reality as me when they took their teen romantic relationships so seriously. Kissing someone wasn't necessarily going to push them up into the inner sphere for me. I've always been quite resistant to that binary of the friendship versus the intimate relationship, and I think the start of the first lockdown in Melbourne really revived that resentment in me.'

Wait? What did Melbourne's first lockdown in 2020 have to do with relationships, sexual, romantic or platonic? That's a rhetorical question, of course, as you'll know if you've been in a lockdown of any length anywhere in the world. They have everything to do with relationships, exposing weaknesses, strengthening bonds, amplifying despair, loneliness and/or stoicism. One of Jinghua's articles at the time, for MTV, particularly piqued my interest: *How Coronogamy (Coronavirus-Induced Monogamy) Has Changed My Sex Life.*

For those who were happily and faithfully in a monogamous relationship with someone living under the same roof during lockdown, things weren't necessarily easy. But for those living alone, unhappily plastered to someone, or with a partner or partners elsewhere, there were additional layers of complexity.

My partner Kate and I weren't living together in 2020. She lived alone in one suburb while I lived with Jess and our two children the next suburb over. None of the four permitted reasons to leave home – shopping for food, outdoor exercise, medical care/caregiving, and work that can't be done from home – addressed our situation.

And so, two evenings a week, when my kids were in bed, I'd cycle to Kate's house, racing against the curfew to spend the night there, cycling home in the morning to get breakfast for the kids before starting work and homeschooling. Two evenings a week, and at weekends, Kate would cycle to mine. We were within the permitted travel radius – the 4.71 kilometres between our houses left us nearly 300 metres to play with – but it crossed my mind more than once that we could get into strange legal waters.

My main sensations and observations riding between households in those evenings of pre-vaccination darkness were that the plants, trees and flowers in gardens and on nature strips had an almost overwhelming aroma due to the near absence of traffic or people, that I was putting on weight given my daily work commute of 20 km on the bike had evaporated, and that I'd feel embarrassed if I had to explain myself to the police.

Yes, I'm going to see my partner. I live back up that way, with my wife. My partner will come back with me in the morning as she's helping my wife and me with our garden.

'It just felt like all of our relationships were supposed to collapse into "essential" and that the only ones that mattered were within your household,' Jinghua says. 'I mean, the household is just an address but suddenly it became the primary organising unit of society.

'I appreciate that it was looser and more practical than the nuclear family or marriage, but it's interesting that it was suddenly the only relationship that had any standing. And then there was the idea at some point of the intimate partner you could visit, with the assumption it meant one – you weren't supposed to have a dozen of them. And then there was the vague provision for care, which I think some people took quite liberally and others took in a very strict way.

'When I wrote in the "coronogamy" article that I felt pushed into monogamy, that was never explicit, it was never policy. When the first lockdown happened, I had a partner I lived with and some very casual relationships with people I was seeing, so it just seemed natural those relationships were going to end – they weren't people on my emergency contact list. If I wasn't going to see my parents or closest friends, it wouldn't make sense to see this or that person.'

What Jinghua is touching on, I think, is a sense of doing the right thing under the circumstances, changing eir behaviour for what seemed valid and sensible health and public safety reasons. As ey wrote in the coronogamy article, this felt 'fair but still uncomfortable':

> It feels very much like some ways of looking after each other are more acceptable than others. So that's the awkward context in which I am effectively experiencing monogamy for the first time. There's a lot of advice out there for people who are 'opening up' their relationship – not so much, it seems, for what to do if you're 'closing down'.[23]

It's intriguing to me that Jinghua's sense of self was as developed as it seemed to be in eir teenage years. As a parent of one, soon to be two, teenagers, I often wonder what tracks have been laid that will influence the rest of their lives. It sometimes feels like they haven't even thought about their sexuality or gender but I assume they must have. I've talked to them about those things in fairly general terms, they've talked to me about them in the same way. And yet part of me wants them to stay children, to not have to go through too hard a time before discovering that, whoever they love and however they present, it's perfectly fine.

4
Knowing you're different

Teenagerdom can feel horrendous, if not for everyone then for lots of us. For me, it did. Aged 12, I was presented with an award for 'best all-round boy' at my primary school in Aberdeen. From an adult perspective, the school and its surrounds were rough as guts – a granite building stitched like a scab onto one of the city's most wounded neighbourhoods, where families flapped like fish on the poverty line and more than half the kids went hungry.

I have to say, it didn't feel poor or rich to me at 12. It was just my school.

I was shy to the point of full head and neck blushing whenever anyone – even my grandparents, who I adored – talked to me in those days, but I felt liked (or rather, I was unaware it was even possible to be disliked) by my peers. They were them, I was me. I had no enemies. My teacher, Mrs Wilson, liked me a lot and I liked her too. Even when she told me off, there was a friendly glint in her eye that I remember and take comfort from even now.

I'd kissed one girl – Penny – badly, thinking you had to do it like in the old films, with your mouths closed, squishing your faces together and moving your heads about while making an *mmmm* sound. Another girl – Syreeta – wanted to kiss me too, but we never did. I wish we had. She told me everything I knew about sex, which up until that point was very little.

Everything changed in the space of a year. By 13, I'd lost my virginity and had started drinking and taking drugs. I'd run away from home twice, skipped school most days, and been in trouble with the police for punch-ups and vandalism. By 14, I had left school for good, with no qualifications, to become a painter and decorator's apprentice at £25 a week.

A few factors played into this. My family had moved to a new part of the city – a better-off area that was ostensibly a step up for us. Apart from my older sister, I knew nobody at the new school. On day one, I slipped on a nasty comment from one of the many school bullies and fell into a vat of heart-freezing, skin-burning insecurity.

Having to make friends while being chronically shy isn't impossible. My eldest son is shy, although not to the same degree as me. He started high school last year and, like me, knew nobody because we'd moved house and catchment areas. I was anxious on his behalf, while acting as if everything would be fine. And it was. Within days, he'd connected with a group of lovely friends. Before I drove them to laser tag one weekend, my son asked me not to say anything in the car (ah, the discomfort of those years) so I didn't, which gave me a good chance to listen. He and his two friends giggled like Beavis and Butthead at things that were deliciously, almost pastorally, innocent: a teacher shushing them for whispering in class, the time an older kid threw a juice box from a bridge and it nearly hit one of them. It was a relief.

In my case, I sensed a threat of violence from a few of the boys in my class. It terrified me – their eagerness to cut people down, to make cruel jokes behind their backs, the implication that they would, could, and maybe even should punch you in the face or do that weird thing men do where they puff out their chests like pigeons and bash into you as a means of intimidation. Their alpha status wasn't up for debate, meaning their sass could never be given back. As an adult, I've walked through boarded-up housing schemes in Glasgow at midnight, through the darkened back streets of Rio de Janeiro before dawn, have spent time – albeit as a visitor – in a Bolivian prison, but nothing has filled me with more dread than those days at school in Aberdeen.

The boys were part of a bigger group that had gone to the same school as each other previously – an army, or at least a battalion, in my adolescent mind. I cowered from them while growing ever more desperate for their approval.

A similar see-saw dynamic was playing out at home. I had a close and happy relationship with my mum – at least until the cops came knocking for the first time. Things were more complicated with my dad. Back then, he would have been known as 'strict', and that's how I thought of him. Now, we'd call it 'abusive'.

With my own kids, I can count on one hand how many times I've slapped them on the back of theirs – in fact, I could count it on two fingers. They remind me of it, periodically: 'You're a terrible dad – you hit my hand that time ...' I'm flooded with sadness and guilt every time they say it which – of course, in the moment – is what they want.

My impulse originally was to tell them about the kicks and punches I received from my own dad. But they don't need to hear that, certainly not yet, and in many ways it's beside the point: I shouldn't be hitting my kids, even a controlled hand slap at a time of acute childhood naughtiness. I think Jess must have told them once, though, because the last time he brought it up, my youngest said he knew my dad used to be 'bad' to me.

And then, exerting what can feel like another type of violence during adolescence, there are hormones: that pipeline of souped-up emotions, flowing into an engine that's not quite ready for the extra torque.

It's discomforting for me – especially looking at my own kids – to think that I felt under pressure to become sexually active at 13, as if I'd left it too long already and needed to grow up. The first time I tried, I failed. I had no idea what I was meant to be doing. Bodies moved on top of each other, right? You're supposed to push, yeah? The second attempt, with a girl slightly older and more experienced than me, went much better.

In terms of sexuality, I was safely heterosexual, it seemed. The alternative – being gay – was to be avoided at all costs and policed accordingly. I remember my mum and grandma in our kitchen, giggling at something I'd done, saying: 'Do you think he's gay?'. I remember my mum being fine with the Marilyn Monroe posters all over my bedroom walls because – leaving aside Monroe's status as a bona fide gay icon – it meant 'at least he's not gay' (although in truth I was obsessed with her femininity rather than her sexiness, but I suppose they were connected. I loved how she sang, played that ukulele and, maybe more than any of those, how she moved).

I remember – was barely allowed to forget – that my sister used to dress me in her clothes, the taunting for which I still think of every time I wear Kate's dresses, make-up and hotpants, which is, frankly, as often as I can (Jack Lemmon and Tony Curtis dressing as Josephine and Daphne in *Some Like it Hot* were as much of a buzz for me as Monroe). Back then, being enthusiastically 'not gay' seemed so completely integral to survival that my mind and body, even though it might have enjoyed it, refused to go there.

I remember my dad making homophobic jokes – or more often camp impersonations of gay people based on the one or two stereotype characters on TV shows such as *Are You Being Served?* – and people, including me, laughing. I remember the kids at school would call everything that was undesirable for boys – singing, crying, dancing, colourful clothes, hairstyles that strayed from the norm – 'gay'. I remember the poor boy who actually *was* gay, who operated as part punch-bag and part scarecrow to warn all others that the flock had to stay together and peck others' eyes out to save their own.

With a time machine, I'd go back and stick up for that boy, apologise for my complicity, for the impressions I did of him to make others laugh, much as my dad had done at home. I felt relieved by his relative weakness and would have pushed him into a puddle if it came to it, to hide my own. I hope that his life improved from that point, that he's still around, that he loves and is dearly loved.

○ ○ ○

In their 2023 book *Personal Score*, award-winning Mununjali Yugambeh poet and author Ellen van Neerven writes about the dedication they had to playing soccer as a teenager and young person, a love that continued until a recent injury.

'There are lots of queer dynamics within the clubs that I played with that I put in the book,' they say. 'I wanted to give the reader a little bit of the atmosphere of what it's like to play in teams where there might be a bit of homophobia alongside a bit of sexual tension between teammates. Or it might even be a full-on affair between teammates that blows the whole team apart.'

'I remember just thinking that there wasn't much writing about sport from a queer perspective. Traditional sports writing is based on professional athletes and is very curated and clean. The things I wanted to write about were dirtier and more complicated.'

As we chat, Ellen agrees that sport, in Australia just as elsewhere, is a particularly charged arena of transphobia, homophobia and racism.

'Absolutely, yeah,' they say. 'I grew up with all sorts of remarks and behaviour being seen as "normal" sledging. I went to a high school that had a soccer program – it was mostly boys with just me and one or two girls.

'There was definitely a vibe of preying on the weak. My class was just so out of control – it was really like *Lord of the Flies*.

'It would be very commonplace to hear someone call someone a dyke or say something transphobic on the field, as well as racial stuff about Indigenous people or people of colour who you were playing against or who were in your team. Nobody would really do anything about it except for the occasional fight. The person receiving the abuse wouldn't laugh it off but the people around them would – they'd say, "Yeah, it's just a joke," or whatever.

'In some ways, you'd expect that would give you tough skin if you're on the receiving end, but not always.

'When I was about 15 and started playing football with adult women, I'd hear a lot of stuff like, "It's such a shame this sport is so full of lesbians," or, "I'm so glad we don't have any lesbians in our team". And I was sort of going, "Oh, OK, well, don't look at me too closely …".'

Of course, racism and homophobia can and do coalesce.

'Certainly, when they're combined, it can be more demoralising,' Ellen says. 'If someone calls you a bitch, then sure – I think everyone's been a called a bitch at some point in their lives. But if, for example, someone calls you a "Blak bitch" that's a bit more targeted and it can really affect you, like: "Oh, shit, you're not just insulting me – you're insulting my family".'

It would be nice, but inaccurate, to suggest those problems have disappeared.

'I think it's still bad now because I go to my brother's games and hear some of those same things,' they say. 'But in terms of going to a women's game, I think it's a much nicer environment these days. But yeah, it still persists, and we still have clubs and people saying: "I don't know how to do anything about it when it's so widespread".'

○ ○ ○

Holden Sheppard is one of Australia's most respected and popular young writers, whose YA novels *Invisible Boys* and *The Brink* are read by adults and the yoof alike. To call them 'gay novels' would be reductive, but they do feature characters who are gay.

His larger-than-life social media presence – selfies featuring a ripped bod, with guns barrelling outwards from a tight guernsey or naked torso – give the impression of someone who feels comfortable in his own skin. As he should. But maybe because of that, I was struck extra hard by a blog post he wrote in 2021 – *I Am Not the Role Model You're Looking For* – in which he describes his teenage experiences and discomfort with being held up as any kind of 'pure' or 'perfect' example to follow:

> I was a big homo. I nearly killed myself because I grew up in a place, time, culture, class, religion, and family setting where homosexuality was a shameful thing. But also, I kept that stuff – what the world around me had deemed evil and sinful – hidden and private.[24]

When I ask Holden about this, he gives a broad-strokes overview of his early years in Western Australia. 'So, you're growing up in a small town where there are no visible gay people,' he says. 'It's a really blokey working-class vibe. My dad was in earth moving and I worked for him as a labourer. My uncles were bricklayers. That was my world – there was nothing beyond that.

'I'm half-Italian – my family's Sicilian – so you hear the word "finocchio", which is "fennel" but also means "faggot". I went to Catholic school, and then to church every week, with all these reminders that homosexuality is a sin.'

His teenage sexual awakening, for all those reasons, came with an ingrained understanding that being same-sex attracted was 'the worst possible thing' he could be.

'But of course, I'm full of hormones,' he says. 'So, I'm watching the footy and thinking, "Well, you know, last week I just thought it was a good game of footy, and now I'm thinking, "Look at all these fucking hot guys". It was wild.'

He took solace, he says, from the assumption that his gayness wouldn't last. 'From age 14 to 16, I was like, "It doesn't really matter, it's normal, everyone goes through it, it's just a phase. When I'm 16 I'll like tits and pussy and I'll be normal".

'And then, when I got to 16, I was like, "Oh shit, this isn't kicking in – I'm not getting the straight hormones". I mean, I had them a little – I've always been bi-curious – but I was overwhelmingly homosexual. It was really difficult when I realised I couldn't get rid of it or control it.'

Looking at the Holdens of then and now, it's tempting to suggest he reached a point where he couldn't hide who he was any more and burst out into the world with pride and self-confidence, but that would be a gross simplification of his own story and that of many others.

'There are beats, places where men have sex with men at night – public toilets, parks, wherever,' he says. 'A lot of the guys who frequent beats are married and their identity is "I'm straight – I've got a wife and kids, a job, I'm never going to break that. But I like having sex with men".

'When I was younger, I was one of them – single and childless, but straight-identified and exploring sex with men in a way that I felt wouldn't complicate my masculinity, my sense of being a bloke. There's a huge spectrum of guys who are homosexual, bisexual or bi-curious but keep it private for various reasons, and it's rarely seen. When it is, on TV or in the media, it's problematised, like, "Here's this guy who just needs to come to terms with himself".

'But these guys *are* being themselves. There's a reason a lot of guys from working-class backgrounds don't come out, and it's not just because they don't want to accept their sexuality. They're accepting enough of it to go and fuck other men. But in some cultures and classes, the idea of being 'gay' inherently takes away your masculinity. So these guys are actually thinking, "I really prefer to be seen as a man, and that's more important to me, and my sense of feeling OK, than coming out".'

Leading a secret life can be less than ideal for those involved or indirectly impacted, of course, but Holden still sympathises.

'I sometimes feel like an oddity – a rough trade guy who ended up falling in love with a guy and came out when he shouldn't have. But I did, and I'm happier now.

'That said, I still think there's so much complexity there beyond all men who experience any same-sex attraction being universally told, "Just accept you're gay and come and join us on the rainbow float". I don't think it's that simple.'

○○○

Julie Peters was in her late thirties before she turned up to work as Julie Peters. She's been with the ABC since 1971, as a camera operator and in various behind-the-scenes roles on iconic programs such as *Countdown* and *Adventure Island*. For her first nineteen years there she presented as a man, transitioning in 1990 – a move that was extremely rare at the time and carried plenty of risk. As she recalled in an ABC profile about her life and career in 2022:

> When I transitioned, one of the guys [at work] said to me: "You should have transsexual tattooed on your forehead so blokes like me aren't tricked into being poofters."[25]

By that point, Julie had been dressing as a woman at work parties for a few years to 'test the water' and was gambling on the fact her growing seniority in her career would help her keep her job.

'I knew they'd be too embarrassed to actually sack me,' she says, 'But in those first six months, I got a huge amount of negative pressure from many of the males I worked with. What was really gratifying, though, was that so many of the women I worked with would tell them off for abusing me.

'It's true that one man wanted to tattoo "transexual" onto my head but it's also worth remembering this was 33 years ago and I was 33 years cuter than I am now. I looked quite similar to the type of woman he found attractive, and I think it confused his subconscious and made him angry at me. Over time, there have been an awful lot of straight guys who kill trans women – or, if not killing them, bashing them – and I think it's often because they find them attractive. I've always been very, very careful in testing to see where somebody's transphobia is before I go much beyond talking to them, let alone dating them.'

Julie has been integral to many of the trans-positive policies and attitudes at the ABC in the decades since, and points to the fact the organisation offers transition leave as a tangible sign of progress – and certainly a welcome shift from the way things were in the early '90s.

'Some people deemed being trans a disorder,' she says. 'For lots of other people, it was just seen as an aspect of being a gay male. The "out" trans women I knew at the time were nearly all sex workers or show-girls and I just saw both of those as extremely high-stress choices that I couldn't cope with psychologically. At the other extreme, I knew some trans women who were very high "stealth" – that was the term people used at the time – and I couldn't cope with that either. Gender nonconformist people are nonconformist in their own way and, by 1990, the force pushing me to find my own way of being was getting very heavy.'

Julie's uncomplicated view of her identity as a child – 'I just thought my parents were dumb for not realising I was a girl' – turned to rage in late primary school and to depression in her teens and early adulthood as the gap between who she was and who she seemed to be grew wider.

'From grade three to grade six, I was extremely angry at the world and I was self-harming,' she says. 'I just couldn't figure out a way to be to be my authentic self, particularly, you know, in 1960s Australia. I don't think we even had a TV at that stage, let alone internet, so there was no way to find out any other way of identifying. When I went through puberty, I realised "This is going to be almost impossible for anybody to believe I'm a woman".'

As the eldest of nine in a Catholic family which had already set her up for life as a priest, there was no guilt-free way to get round the 'sin' of being a girl in a boy's body, no social support of the sort she would have needed, and little chance she would have sought help in any case, such was her confusion and fear.

'As I got older, it made me crazy and I started drink driving, which is basically chronic suicide – you're attempting slowly to kill yourself. As a 20-year-old, I was eligible to be sent to Vietnam, as our right-wing government put it, to "fight communists and save the free world". I thought it would be a slight relief to go and get shot so I wouldn't have to put up with it all.

'But then it clicked for me that I didn't actually want to die. And that's when I gave myself permission to start my identity quest and find my way of being. I understand that, on a biological level, I can never be a woman, but culturally, I am a woman in that people will relate to me as a woman.'

Julie's 2016 PhD thesis – *A Feminist Post-transsexual Autoethnography on Challenging Normative Gender Coercion* – was written with the aim of helping health professionals deal with their trans clients. Despite the academic title, it reads in certain chapters like the best, most engrossing memoir. A sample:

> Mum's theory that there were two genders and that boys grew up to be men seemed so unreasonable that I was sure she was wrong, and so I was constantly on the lookout for exceptions. According to my uncle, who was a farmer, sheep were divided differently: into lambs, ewes, rams and wethers. When I questioned him further, he told me wethers used to be boys. Of course, I then thought that if sheep could be used to be boys, then maybe human boys can change from boys to something else. I started to interrogate him about how sheep changed from boys to wethers, but he suddenly seemed a little

embarrassed and wouldn't tell me. I still took it as proof that just because you are a boy doesn't necessarily mean you need stay one.[26]

These days, Julie thinks about her life as a series of discreet but connected stories. 'There are many, many versions,' she says. 'It's very context-dependent. Like, if I go to the supermarket, most people just take me as some boring woman doing the shopping. My identity is based on everything I've done up until now.'

○ ○ ○

Dr Arlie Alizzi is a Yugambeh writer, editor and curator who has written on Indigenous transgender issues, and on race, colonialism and sexuality more broadly. He points out that 'new' identities happen gradually rather than all at once.

'Everybody who knows me, or knows my private life, knows me as a trans person,' he says. 'But that's not been a unified process – it's been multi-stage. One of my cousins came out a couple of years ago and it was a much quicker process. Everyone in the family was informed. My process has been a little bit more private.'

Identifying openly, or even privately, as trans can be dictated to some degree by access to healthcare and an individual's financial position, Arlie says, but also by other more personal hurdles. 'For me, it's definitely also psychological. People take their time reaching a comfort level with their own identity. It might take five, six, seven years, during which they'll claim, if they're trans, they don't want to transition – or they'll go back and forth on that. In my case, I've experienced some mental blocks.'

A lot has changed in the ten or so years since Arlie started identifying as trans. While transphobia still thrashes around like an almighty shit hose, there's also more visibility, support and public advocacy for trans people.

'I think it's a mainstreaming thing,' he says. 'When I was writing about transness in 2015, I observed the more bureaucratic elements of trans acceptance and trans culture coming up. In Victoria, we saw the establishment of a Gender and Sexuality Commissioner in 2015, and the adoption of things like the International Day Against Homophobia, Biphobia, Interphobia and Transphobia. There's definitely more language and culture around transness now.'

It's been meaningful for Arlie to engage with the work of Brotherboys and Sistergirls – movements and frames of reference that grew out of sexual health conferences run by Aboriginal medical associations in partnership with the AIDS Trust of Australia in the 1990s.

The terms Sistergirls and Brotherboys are used for and by trans and gender diverse people in some Aboriginal and Torres Strait Islander communities. As the author Hayden Moon wrote in Junkee in 2020:

> 'Sistergirl' and 'Brotherboy' are very inclusive terms, as they are trans identities that accept everyone, including those who don't separate themselves from the gender they were assigned at birth.
>
> So, a First Nations person who has a feminine spirit but was assigned male at birth (AMAB) might identify as a Sistergirl. This means she could be anywhere on the gender spectrum from a feminine gay man, to a non-binary person, to a trans woman (and vice versa). A Brotherboy may have a boy spirit and therefore identify as a Brotherboy, but not identify as a "man".[27]

Reading the report from the First National Indigenous Sistergirl Forum, held in Queensland in 1999, was something of an eye-opener for Arlie. Billed as 'A forum for all Indigenous people who identify as sistergirl or have transgender qualities', the write-up from the event formed a bridge to the not-too-distant past.

'It's interesting to me how amnesiac our queer culture is,' Arlie says. 'There's so much we don't know because we don't have a working connection to the generation – let alone two or three generations – before us. I was still in school when the Sistergirls conference happened and had no awareness of what queer and trans people in our country were living through in the 1970s and '80s. If I'd known this stuff in my twenties, when I became polyamorous and started having my own period of growth, I think I would have been a little less arrogant. We're not inventing this stuff for the first time.'

Even if it hadn't made Arlie or any other young person less conceited, a sense of cross-generational continuity would have at least shown people they weren't alone.

'When you grow up queer, depending on where you are and who you're friends with, you don't necessarily have access to that generation above,' he says. 'You have to do a lot of work to go and find those people, and then even more work to feel connected with them, if you're lucky. I think more can be done to normalise that kind of dialogue. The type of work done by the Sistergirls for over 30 years, where we name our identities but also discuss those identities as functional things, has been really important.'

○○○

It can be a struggle to see which patterns have formed in your life and even harder to get a sense of how those patterns came to be.

I started seeing a therapist in 2017 at Kate's gentle, then not so gentle, insistence. I'm every bit the stereotypical male, and my Scottish sense of grimace-and-bear-it masculinity is overlaid with the Australian version from the quarter of my life I've lived here. I don't like going to the doctor because I'm squeamish and avoidant. I didn't like the idea of seeking help for mental health as that would have clearly suggested – and even worse, *shown* – I wasn't coping.

I was exhausted from trying to maintain two simultaneous adult romantic relationships, from trying to find as much quality time as I could for my kids, from working in an office forty to fifty hours a

week, from writing – or trying to find time to write – in my (non-existent) free time. Where in the past I'd been able to enjoy my low points
in private, I found myself with no alone time and had to have my low
points in company. Eyes were on me at all times, as were ears when
I mentioned for the first time I wanted to die. I mean, I didn't. But
I wanted everything to stop and my brain's way of dealing with that
was to suggest a whole raft of ways that I could end myself. Still, a
therapist? Surely I could handle things on my own.

In that same period, I read an article published on the University
of Melbourne's *Pursuit* website which – paired with Kate's growing
insistence I see someone – changed my view. It was about a large-scale
empirical research project looking at men and the societal attitudes
influencing their behaviour. The bit I remember most is this:

> The study of almost 14,000 Australian men found that those who
> strongly identified with being self-reliant, a trait traditionally associ-
> ated with maleness, were significantly more likely to report thoughts
> of suicide or self-harm.[28]

The main thing I knew about therapy was that you were supposed to
speak, ideally in a New York accent, so I spoke:

I had no time for myself. I was doing everything I could to keep others
happy and it still wasn't enough. I was deep in time and affection debt
and feeling the squeeze of compound interest. Kate wanted more from
me, felt – as I did – it was her due. Jess wanted more from me, felt – as
I did – it was fair. My kids wanted more time with me, felt – or maybe
only I did – they hardly saw me anymore. The spinning plates stage
had passed; I was on the floor in a pile of smashed crockery. Sometimes it felt like my heart was stopping; other times that it wanted
to claw its way out of my chest. I worried for my kids. Worried that
Jess and I were sleepwalking through the end of our marriage. Was
annoyed she was falling for other people. Annoyed I'd fallen in love
with Kate. Annoyed that it was all so noisy and bright and sharp-
edged. What was I doing? What was polyamory anyway? A stupid

word to describe a daft concept for people who were too witless to settle for monogamy.

At some point, as I was talking about my teenage years, I mentioned my girlfriend's name from that time, Naomi. And then changed that to Jane. Or was it Gemma? Actually, it was all three. I mean, we were kids so there was no chance of us moving in together and spending our weekends at Ikea, but they were my girlfriends all the same. We kissed, held hands, had sex. I talked later in the same session about Alexandra, my partner at university, how well she got on with Petra, who I was also seeing periodically, but not so much Lucia.

I was as surprised by the therapist's comment as she seemed to be by my stunned reaction when she said, in a rare lull: 'So, you've always been polyamorous?'

5
Coming out

The author Andrea Goldsmith lives quite close to me – a proverbial stone's throw, in fact – and she's invited me to her house for our interview.

I'm excited by this prospect – but with Melbourne's Covid numbers rising again, we've agreed it's probably safer to meet virtually. So here we are on a humid, doom-scrolly Monday afternoon, not sharing crackers and cheese but peering at each other through the smudgy windows of our webcams.

I've just finished reading Andrea's 2019 book *Invented Lives*, her eighth novel, and have taken copious notes about its characters and their complex relationships with each other and themselves.

The protagonist, Galina Kogan, is a Russian Jewish émigré in Australia and the story itself is something of a Russian doll: Galina's feelings of loss for her recently deceased mother nestle within her sense of not belonging in Melbourne which, in turn, nestles within her and other characters' need to maintain personas that hide essential facets of their sexuality and lives.

I intend to ask Andrea about this, and about her relationship with the late poet Dorothy (Dot) Porter, about how it feels to be described regularly – without asking or agreeing to be – as a 'lesbian author', and how attitudes may or may not have changed towards same-sex attracted people over the course of her lifetime.

What I hadn't bargained for, but probably should have given the astuteness of Andrea's writing, is how probing and curious she'd be. 'I know you're interviewing me, but ...' she says more than once. She asks how I feel about Jess having other partners (it's complicated), how she and Kate get on with each other (pretty well, actually), and how our relationship(s) fit or elbow their way into the tapestry of our broader families.

In my own case, my mum is dead and my dad and I have never spoken about it because he's unwell and struggles with even the slightest change in circumstances. I'm not afraid of how he would react towards me (those days are gone) – I'd just like to tell him in person, when I can be with him for a while to make sure he's OK, and not over the phone from Australia. But my mum would have loved Kate, I'm sure of that, and vice versa. I'm guessing she'd have been concerned for my kids at the start, and again now, years later, that my marriage is ... well, more on that later.

Jess's mum and step-dad have always invited Kate to family get-to-gethers and tried – successfully, I think – to make her feel welcome, as have Jess's siblings. Has it been weird seeing me rock up to barbeques and birthday bashes with my partner *and* my wife? Probably. That's always felt weird to me too.

Jess's dad, the first time he met Kate, brought her a Lego set as a gift, which was a little unexpected, maybe, but a sign of his affection, a peace offering that I like to think symbolised the opportunity to build something new and exciting.

Kate's parents are practising Roman Catholics with an active role in the church which, on the face of it, sounds conservative with a capital C. I was uncomfortable the first time we met, could only see myself through their eyes – or rather, my own inward-turning peep-ers: there I was, eating their food and guzzling their wine, a married man with children, the shortest of short straws in what they would have wanted for their youngest daughter.

But since the start, they've invited Jess, me and the boys over for Christmas dinner with Kate and her siblings, giving gifts to my kids just as they do with their other two grandchildren, keeping up with our news, telling us theirs, laughing and topping up our glasses.

If it was the 1970s, I'd be tempted to make a joke about the misfortune of having two mothers-in-law, but the truth is I'm enamoured of them both, as I am with my three de facto dads-in-law. I'm an immigrant who, in a practical sense, has been orphaned for years, so family connectedness – in whatever shape it comes – is welcome.

'It's so interesting to hear that about Kate's parents,' Andrea says. 'When people are exposed to ways of being that are not their own, but they like the people and meet them within a family setting, they often find in themselves an acceptance that surprises everyone.'

'I think of my father, who was a man of his time – he was born in 1919. We had a close relationship, but I'd never discussed my sexuality with him, I felt I couldn't, I was sure he wouldn't understand. I'd been with men and I'd been with women and he'd been very attached to my former partner.

'When Dot came into my life, he said to me one day: "Darling, do you really think she's the one for you?" And I thought: "Oh my god, this is my father." He'd known this about me, but we'd never talked about it. In that moment, he was telling me that he loved me and wanted my happiness – and because he was my dad, he was also putting in his two-cents worth.

'There's always the possibility for people like my father or your in-laws to open up in ways they might not have previously.'

Of course, there's also the possibility they won't, which is why the stakes can feel so high.

○ ○ ○

Filip Vukašin's 2021 novel *Modern Marriage* follows a woman, Klara, who discovers her recently deceased husband had been sleeping with men, a secret he had also kept from his homophobic birth family in Melbourne. Her co-worker, Tomas, also gay, reflects on how hard it had been to come out to his family in South America:

> How worried he was about his parents' friends finding out in Peru, how scared he was to tell Klara and others at uni, how frightening it was to think that he might not get an intern job or that his Australian visa might be rejected if someone found out. Some of it was paranoia, some of it was reality.[29]

My own most pressing worry when I meet Filip at Abbotsford Convent in Melbourne is that I'm drenched in sweat, my hair plastered to my face. I've ridden back and forth along bike paths getting lost and swearing at Siri and the Google Maps person, running later and becoming more flustered with every brake and about-turn.

Filip, when I finally arrive, is the picture of calm, his warm smile and immediately calming bedside manner surely a credit to him in his day job as a doctor. As sweat pools at the base of my spine, we order coffee, talk about the warm weather, the food options and, in time, coming out.

'When I was in the closet, it was hard,' he says. 'I'd go out with friends, and we'd end up in gay clubs. But I wasn't quite there yet so I felt uncomfortable even though I wanted to be there. It was such a mish-mash of emotions.'

The 'being gay' part was one thing – the dishonesty another. 'You know, I'm supposed to be this person who is a good son, a good brother, a diligent worker, and I'm lying … that never sat well with me.'

Aged 29, he met Matt, a psychotherapist who in time would become his husband – their deepening relationship a catalyst for Filip to speak with his parents.

'I sat them down and said, "Look, I have something to tell you," he remembers. 'It was too hard for me to say "I'm gay", so I said, "I have a boyfriend".

'I'd lined up everything just in case. I knew I could afford to live on my own. I had a career and supportive friends. I made sure of all that because you hear so many horror stories.

'But they were like: "Oh god, is that all? I thought you were going to tell us you were dying."

'I was crying, with all these snot bubbles, and they're like, "It's fine, it's OK".

'I'd built up this idea that they were going to be monstrous and disown me but it was the opposite.

'One of their first questions was, "When are we going to meet him?". It was really healing just to finally be honest and show them who I am.'

ooo

As part of the *Queerstories* podcast series hosted by the writer and performer Maeve Marsden, author Benjamin Law gave a funny but stark reminder that the first 'coming out', however cathartic, is rarely the last. He told his mother initially, he says, after which:

'I came out to my older siblings. Then my younger siblings. A few years later, I came out to my dad. Then I'd come out to taxi drivers. And hotel reservation staff. New colleagues. Extended relatives. Some arsehole taking my order. Because coming out, I think a lot of people in this room know, isn't a single moment. Queers spend our entire lives coming out.'[30]

Author, editor and researcher Roz Bellamy knows this as well as anybody. We first made contact in 2020 when Roz commissioned a piece by me for *Archer Magazine* – which they edit – about being polyamorous. Here's a snippet:

> Coming out as polyamorous, in my experience, has been similar to the 14 years I spent coming out as vegetarian: some people are quick to tell me they are too, or would like to be. Others get defensive, as if I'm somehow criticising their life choices (I'm not), or say it makes no difference to them ... and then invite me round for dinner less frequently.[31]

As variously – and simultaneously – lesbian, bisexual and non-binary, Roz has endured and celebrated several coming-outs, as explored in their 2023 memoir *Mood* which, among other things, delves into their time working as a high-school teacher in Melbourne.

'I happened to be teaching at a school that had anti-Semitism, homophobia and transphobia manifesting in quite ugly, aggressive ways,' they say. 'Being a Jewish queer teacher in that environment, while at the same time trying to make sense of my gender identity, became this really strange daily struggle.

'I was constantly thinking about which bits of myself to share and which bits to hide. By the time I started teaching, I was extremely out of the closet but also feeling I needed to go back into it for some parts of me. I found myself navigating issues I hadn't worried about since I was a baby queer.'

Coming out as lesbian in 2004 was 'definitely the hardest,' Roz says, due to their age at the time, the complexity of dealing with reactions from their family and their partner's, and the 'hostile' view of homosexuality propagated by their Orthodox Jewish school.

They knew they were bisexual but didn't identify openly as such until a decade later, in 2014. 'I was 20 for the big coming out and 30 when I came out as bisexual – god knows what's coming at 40,' Roz says. 'I'm clearly getting quicker though because coming out as non-binary happened a bit sooner.'

The more recent coming out, they say, is 'still being navigated' – a process that started with a moment of self-recognition in 2018 and continues to be a 'rollercoaster'.

'I feel like coming out as bi was just a little amendment to coming out as lesbian,' they say. 'Coming out as non-binary was like starting the process all over again because it was about gender rather than sexuality. Australia's much further behind on gender than it is on sexuality – not that I think it's all positive with sexuality. But at least people seem to equate sexuality with urges and attraction and desire. With gender and transness, it still seems to be "there's something wrong with that person" – basically, psychopathologising them.'

That diversity in sexuality and gender expression can still be taken as a sign of mental disorder feels, to say the least, outdated.

Legally, Australia has taken significant steps to distance itself from those attitudes. The Marriage Amendment Act in 2017 was – for better or worse – a 'normalising' step, particularly for those gay and lesbian people who were partnered and nominally monogamous. Essentially, that amendment erased an Act introduced by the Howard Government in 2004 that explicitly prevented same-sex marriages. A same-sex reform package passed through Parliament in 2008, allowing for gay and lesbian de facto couples to have the same rights – including in areas such as citizenship, superannuation, social security and tax – as opposite-sex de facto couples.

There have been other wins, in a legal sense, along the way.

The Sex Discrimination Act (1984) made it unlawful to discriminate against a person:

because of their sex, gender identity, sexual orientation, marital or relationship status, family responsibilities, because they are pregnant or might become pregnant or because they are breastfeeding.[32]

The wording and principles at play are a far cry from the British *Buggery Act 1522*, inherited by pre-federation Australia, which until 1890 rendered sodomy a crime punishable by death. But alternate versions of that Act persisted until relatively recently.

As already mentioned, decriminalisation of sex between men in Australia (it was never illegal for women) began in South Australia in 1975 and ended in Tasmania in the late '90s. There are plenty of places in the world where it remains a crime with severe penalties, including imprisonment and execution.

Progress, regression and the social and procedural attitudes informing them are slow at times, sudden at others, asynchronous always. The ire and hysteria directed at trans and gender-diverse people in Australia and elsewhere in recent times is depressingly reminiscent of that shown to gay and lesbian people in the near past (and continuing present) – a bigotry, like all bigotry, that forgets or wilfully ignores the most open of all open secrets: we're all human.

Church, state and psychiatry have played their part in urging people to set aside that universal truth. The *Diagnostic and Statistical Manual of Mental Disorders* included 'homosexuality' as a disease and/or disorder until the 1980s. Conversion therapy – which has historically involved techniques such as injecting LGBT people with drugs and administering electric shocks to 'correct' them – was only outlawed in Victoria in 2021,[33] following similar bans in Queensland and the ACT. Its proponents would have us disregard the fact it leads to no lasting change in 'patients', other than making them feel needlessly worse about themselves than they already did, all the while lending a pseudoscientific sheen to society's toxic pores.

A 2021 study by Western Sydney University found that more than 90 per cent of LGBTQIA+ teenagers at government, independent and Catholic high schools across Australia hear regular homophobic language at school, while nearly 30 per cent have either witnessed or been the victims of physical harassment because of their gender or sexuality.[34]

Even with that context, I wonder why it took Roz a full decade between coming out as lesbian and bi. 'As sad as it sounds, I think it took that long to develop agency,' they say. 'Part of it was societal. At that time, people still couldn't get their heads around being gay or lesbian, let alone bisexual or queer.'

'When I was 30, I started writing more and that really helped – that sense of narrating yourself that non-fiction can offer. But I was also aware that some people see coming out as bisexual as attention-seeking, especially if you dare to come out when you are in a seemingly opposite-sex relationship. There's biphobia in queer and non-queer communities.'

○ ○ ○

'I figured out I was bisexual when I was 14,' Angela Meyer says. 'I mean the word, not the feelings. I was working at a cinema at the time. Before one shift, I started reading an interview with Angelina Jolie, who said she was bisexual. I can't remember the exact quote but it was along the lines of, "I like women, men, big people, small people ..." And I remember feeling this rush of recognition.

'I grew up in regional New South Wales in a working-class family, where there wasn't much exposure to that language, and not much exposure to queer people either. I mean, they would have been there, for sure, but I wasn't aware of them.'

The untainted thrill of Angela's self-recognition lasted a matter of seconds. 'I went immediately to my workmate and told him, "I'm bisexual", and he was like, "Oh, that's hot!"

'That really set me on an interesting track. On one hand, I was accepted immediately but on the other it became a singular way to be accepted. It was all very confusing for me, and still is in some ways.

'When I told some girl friends at school, they were shocked and weirded out, and some people called me "freak".'

Angela told her parents at 20, shortly after her younger sister came out as gay. 'I saw their reaction to that, which was very positive and lovely. I mentioned to them that I was bisexual and nothing much was made of it. I suppose it didn't feel like a big deal for them unless I was going to start dating a woman long-term.'

She didn't identify publicly as bisexual until her thirties, she says, in part because of the 'invisibility of bisexuality when you're in a monogamous relationship, whether it's with someone of the same gender or otherwise'.

Beyond it being a temporary superpower, it's hard to imagine many scenarios in which being invisible would be good. If coming out is the equivalent of dramatically removing a dust sheet from yourself and proclaiming, 'look, world, here I am', the realisation that you're still not seen or acknowledged after doing so must be doubly damaging.

Here's how the writer Misty Gedlinske put it in a 2019 TEDx talk, 'Bisexuality: The Invisible Letter "B"':

> My invisibility powers come from being bisexual and are reinforced by being committed to an opposite-sex partner. [...] The assumption that people make about folk who have opposite-sex partners or who are just not open about their orientation is that we're straight, or heterosexual. [...] When the power of those assumptions combines with the power of fear the results are so strong the affected person can become invisible even to themselves.[35]

Attending the International Bisexuality Research Conference in 2021 gave Angela some useful new hooks on which to hang her experiences.

'One of the researchers was talking about how shame comes from internalised stigma for bi+ people and how, if you internalise that at a young age, it can be very powerful. That was really striking to me because I've had a journey with shame that people often don't understand. In my novel A *Superior Spectre*, the protagonist Jeff has that same kind of shame. When I was writing it, I didn't necessarily think about where that came from but then I realised a lot of it was from me coming out and certain reactions I've had to my sexuality.

'My dad passed away a couple of years ago, which was very sad. Right up to the end, I would interject my bisexuality into the conversation here and there, but it was never the same to him as my sister being gay because I was with a man. You do find yourself having to come out again and again to people, and that can be wearing.'

○○○

Does this chime with Omar Sakr, I wonder, the feeling of being unseen? Yes, it does.

'I put "bisexual" in my Twitter bio and elsewhere because it is in many ways an invisible sexuality by virtue of the fact that most people are in, or seek to be in, monogamous relationships,' he says. 'I had it there when I was single, when I was with men, and still now, as a man married to a cis woman.'

He prefers 'queer' to 'bisexual', in part because 'bisexual' sounds like a medical diagnosis. And also 'because "bi" inevitably brings to mind a binary, which I dislike. There have been efforts recently to say "bi+" as a nod to including other gender identities, but it doesn't do much in my view. In any case, I'm a stubborn, contrary bastard, and I'm beginning to suspect I stick with "bisexual" purely because it is such a contested term on all sides.

'There is no one way, no core bisexual narrative – you couldn't even say, really, what it looks like for any gender, and there's an enormous freedom in that which I value deeply.'

By saying it's contested on all sides, I'm guessing Omar is touching on the biphobia mentioned by Roz ... is that right?

'I'm wary of this topic, to be honest,' he says. 'That's a common insecurity for bisexual people. I think everyone needs to do some serious work on understanding how to deal with their insecurities, and that validation cannot enter us externally, it has to come from within. That said, prejudice against bisexuals is real, and I think it's been driven deeper in recent times by the mainstream campaign for same-sex marriage, which involved sanitising queerness with slogans like *Love is love* and *Born this way*.

'That narrative positions queerness as something that must be accepted because there is no choice, no decision made by the queer person – it's genetic, inevitable, and so on.

'*Born this way* is an inherently conservative argument, and one that goes directly against bisexuality in particular, which is positioned as always being between choices, or as always having the choice to be normative or not "sinful". This generates resentment from cis hetero and homosexual people who, for whatever reason, desire the ability to move between these cultural and social spheres, to be seen as more "exotic" or less, more "dangerous" or less, and so on.

'The reality of course is that we all have this ability, to varying degrees, depending on our race, class, support network, and individual courage.'

OOO

Ellen van Neerven was in their late twenties before they started identifying as non-binary, a decision and process that was far from straightforward.

'When I was a kid, I didn't know that transness existed on a spectrum,' they say. 'I very much saw it as: you're either a boy or a girl. Certainly, there wasn't much trans representation in my life at that time. I just would always feel a little at odds in some ways with things that were going on, and kind of boxed into doing things that were seen as "girly".

'I thought that was all just part of my queerness until I really started to break down that there was a difference between sexuality and gender identity, and that there was option to opt out of being identified as a binary gender. And then I was like, "I think that's me".'

There were people in their life, Ellen says, that were in no way shocked by this, which didn't necessarily make it easier for them to accept about themselves and discuss with others.

'I got to that place in my late 20s, and it came with a lot of internalised stuff that was actually very painful,' they say. 'I had to get through a lot of that on my own, because I was like "I need to figure it out before I can tell people".

'With the first couple of people, I would try to get the words out and would just burst into tears. I was like, "Clearly, there's still a lot that I need to unpack within myself"'.

○ ○ ○

In my case, I'm not only hetero-passing but stubbornly, for the most part, hetero.

When I'm with Jess and the kids we look like a 'normal' family; when I'm with Kate and the kids we look like a 'normal' family; when we're all together we look, I imagine, like a 'normal' family with a sister or female friend in tow. I've never tried – and would probably be punched in the neck if I did – holding both of them by the hand when we're out and about together.

All of which is to say, the coming out part for me, other than with family and close friends, has always been largely optional. I've never felt in any physical danger from people who know or sense my situation.

I've definitely felt judged, though, and know my relationship status was problematic to a previous manager, to some friends, to some of Kate and Jess's friends and colleagues. I've felt awkward when someone has invited me to something with a 'plus one', or when someone who knows my situation automatically invites Jess and not Kate. There are uncertain moments and negative impressions that feel real at the time but later elude me. Nothing that would stand up in court – but still something, goddammit.

In her 2020 book *Polysecure*, the American psychotherapist Jessica Fern suggests the nondescript but troubling feelings I experience are those of 'a man (usually white and cisgender) who is facing not having certain privileges for the first time'.

Such men – i.e. me – have to face:

> the power dynamics that they have participated in and benefited from, [and] the experience of going through a privilege flip can be disorienting, painful and even traumatic. Men can also experience further ostracization when they are met with contention from nonmonogamous communities because they still hold other forms of privilege, and when they experience a lack of support and guidance in how to make sense of the privileges they've lost and those they still hold.' [36]

I like this partly because it rings true and partly because it puts things in perspective. Being a white cisgender heterosexual-identifying man can suck, no question, but if my relatively teeny bit of discomfort has shown me anything it's that others – on an intersecting and sometimes exponential scale – have it far, far worse.

Where Jess and Kate are concerned, I've certainly noticed an insidious and immediate type of male privilege (or confusion) playing out. When some men hear the word 'nonmonogamous', their brains interpret it as 'I'd like to have sex with you and every other person in here immediately and indiscriminately, thank you very much'.

My friend Rochelle Siemienowicz is the author of the 2015 memoir *Fallen*, in which she writes about her strict Seventh-day Adventist upbringing and how that complicated her feelings about many things, including being nonmonogamous. Her novel-in-progress, about a polyamorous family, is informed in part by her 24-year marriage, her concurrent seven-year relationship with another man, and her husband's relationship with another woman.

'I can definitely relate to that idea of men who aren't poly thinking polyamorous women must be open to any man's sexual advances,' she says.

'But I also think some straight, monogamous men can find polyamorous women really threatening, as if we're going to be a bad influence on their wives and partners. Sometimes there's even a certain amount of fear – as if this is the beginning of the end for their regime of having their women all to themselves because, they think, surely every straight woman would want another man if they could.'

Would they though?

'No, not really,' she says. 'Most straight women I know wouldn't want to have to keep more than one man happy. A lot of women have said to me, "I don't know how you have the energy".'

It might be worth noting that polyamory wasn't even a word until the early 1990s, when it was coined by the late author Morning Glory Zell Ravenheart, although nonmonogamy very obviously predates it.

As Christopher Ryan and Cacilda Jethá argue in the 2010 bestseller *Sex At Dawn*:

No group-living nonhuman primate is monogamous, and adultery has been documented in every human culture studied – including those in which fornicators are routinely stoned to death. In light of all of this bloody retribution, it's hard to see how monogamy comes "naturally" to our species. Why would so many risk their reputations, families, careers – even presidential legacies – for something that runs against human nature?[37]

'I actually love the idea of a soulmate,' Rochelle says. 'I'm very attracted to the idea that one person can be your best friend, your lover, your everything – that you're almost merged. But I've found through my life that one person is usually not enough for me and that most people don't want the level of intensity I like.'

Rochelle and I are both of a generation for whom the language required to be open about ethical nonmonogamy as a young adult – and the confidence it would be sympathetically received – ranged from inadequate to non-existent.

'I definitely felt I was outside the norm,' she says. 'There were times I was socially ostracised for being a "slut" or cheating or, you know, two-timing.'

Though comfortable with the polyamorous label now, Rochelle's identity – like everyone else's – is prone to changes over time.

'When I got married the first time, that was always going to be till death do us part,' she says. 'I really meant it when I made my vows. When the sexual part of the relationship broke down, I was looking for a way to maintain that commitment while still being able to have sex, because I was only 21. Nonmonogamy has evolved for me out of the need to honour what I've honestly felt I wanted and needed.'

○○○

RWR (Rob) McDonald, author of *The Nancys* and *Nancy Business*, was 27 when he came out as gay but 'about four' when he knew he was attracted to men. 'I didn't have the words,' he says. 'I just knew men were like "whoa". But I was in denial for a long time and repressed my sexuality.'

In person – we're at a North Melbourne restaurant on a rainy Thursday morning – Rob is as warm as his comedy–crime novels. His books manage to balance stories of grief and grisly murder with infectious charm and positivity, much of which is generated through the characters of Uncle Pike and his boyfriend Devon, guardians of the childhood protagonist, Tippy. The novels' celebration of camp in small-town New Zealand is made possible by Rob's decision to set them in 'a post-homophobic world'.

'I wanted to explore what that might look like,' he says. 'If that was the reality, what would it mean for myself and other people who have gone through homophobia, including their own internalised homophobia?'

At 23, Rob began a relationship with a woman who was 17 years his senior. 'I only mention her age because it meant we were able to negotiate our sexual relationship,' he says. 'I knew I didn't want to go out with a woman romantically because it would feel dishonest unless I was fully into it. But I loved my time with her and leaned so much.

'At that stage, I still hadn't come to terms with being gay but it allowed me that freedom to go, "Well, maybe I'm bisexual". It wasn't until I had a sexual experience with a man that I realised "this feels right, this is what I'm supposed to be doing".'

A few years later, having returned from a period living in London to Invercargill, New Zealand, the pressure was building to come out, to himself as much as anyone else. He'd never told anyone because 'it was scary as fuck'.

'I was at a party trying to cover for a girl whose boyfriend was looking for her, and I said: "I'm gay." That was the first person I'd ever said it to and as soon as I did, I was like: "That's my truth".'

From there, the next steps became clearer if not easier. 'I was about to go up to Auckland but wanted to tell my family first so I could actually start living my life,' he says. 'I told my siblings but couldn't tell my dad because he was away somewhere.

'I wrote him a letter and said I'd call. I told his partner too before leaving so she could help him through it.

'When I rang him that night, he was really disappointed. And then, when he came to Auckland, we went for a drive and he said: "So, are you going to be normal?". And I was like: "I *am* fucking normal".'

'But to my dad's credit, he went through this amazing journey with me, to the point of being a really proud grandparent to my two amazing kids and talking to people about how proud he was of me and them. We started off rocky but that's because he was coming from the same culture that kept me in the closet until I was 27.'

Calling that culture homophobic or bigoted (while probably accurate) requires something most of just love to stick onto ourselves and others: labels.

6
What even are you?

The Australian comedian Hannah Gadsby, in her 2018 Netflix special *Nanette*, says the following:

> I don't lesbian enough, not in the scheme of my existence. If you were to plot my week, not a lot of lesbianing gets done. I cook dinner way more than I lesbian, but nobody ever introduces me as 'that chef comedian', do they?' [38]

It gets a big laugh because, like all good comedy, it comes screaming from an otherwise quiet place of truth. Labels, whether used as an insult, diagnosis, practical measure or point of pride, are always inadequate. If we were to write all the different things we are on post-it notes and stick them to ourselves, we'd struggle to move. Add the labels others have for us, and then, on extra-big post-its, the ones we most want the world to know about us, and we'd keel over. As Gadsby puts it elsewhere in *Nanette*: 'I don't even think that "lesbian" is the right identity fit for me, I really don't. I may as well come out now – I identify as "tired".'

In his groundbreaking 1971 book *Homosexual: Oppression and Liberation*, the Australian academic and pioneering gay rights activist Dennis Altman imagined a future in which labels such as 'gay' and 'straight' would die off as people came to terms with the inherent fluidity of sexuality and gender. [39] Forty-two years later, in his 2013 book

The End of the Homosexual? he conceded that 'the idea of a fluid and diverse sexuality that does not need categories is still utopian'.[40]

Now, nearly a decade after that, we're chatting on Zoom about the LGBTQIA+ abbreviation.

'I've got several problems with it,' he says. 'The first is that it's based on a very Western – indeed a very American – concept of sexuality and gender. It's not particularly useful if one tries to apply it outside of those societies.

'But I also think it pulls together things that are actually quite different. L, G and B are all descriptions of sexual preference or sexual desire. T is, of course, for trans, which is an expression of gender, and may or may not be related to sexual desire. The I – intersex – is a biological reality based on a person's physical characteristics.'

Nevertheless, the letters have come together, signifying words and concepts with changeable natures. 'Lesbian', as a medical term, dates back to the 1890s, although its association with the writer Sappho, from Lesbos in Greece, is obviously much older. An Austro-Hungarian lawyer by the name of Karoly Maria Kertbeny coined 'bisexual' and 'homosexual' in the 1860s – successfully replacing his previous coinage, Urning, to describe same-sex attracted men. 'Gay' – to signify same-sex attracted men, women and all other sexual and gender minorities – reached the mainstream in the 1960s. LGB, to recognise solidarity but also difference, gained ground in the 1980s. Then 'transgender' was added for the same reasons, leading to greater use of LGBT in the 1990s.

In more recent years, queer, intersex and asexual (or "allied" depending on who you ask) have been included to form LGBTQIA+, the now standard plus-sign a recognition that there are categories of non-heterosexual and non-cisgender people still absent. In a bid to deal with that nuance, another term – LGBTQQIP2SAA – is now in use, to signify lesbian, gay, bisexual, transgender, queer, questioning, intersex, pansexual, two spirit, asexual, and ally.

'I prefer the term "queer" as an overall category,' Dennis says. 'I'd rather that than watching the poor newsreaders on SBS struggling every time they have to say "the LGBTQIA+ community". For that reason, if nothing else, I think "queer" is a very useful word.'

Less useful, in a practical sense, is queer theory, he says, which has 'become a very successful branch of a certain sort of wanky academia'.

'An awful lot of it is written in language that's pretty impenetrable if you haven't done academic work in cultural or gender studies. It's ironic that people who want to be supportive of activists write in a way that most activists can't understand.'

I find talking to Dennis refreshing and sometimes alarming. Knowing he's an internationally recognised activist with a prominent role throughout the 1980s and '90s in government and community responses to HIV/AIDS in Australia and overseas, I suppose I'd expected him to be automatically in favour of certain things. In my mind, I'd labelled him as a 'gay left-wing academic', and – if I'm honest – tend to imagine gay left-wing academics as being (genuinely or for the sake of diplomacy) supportive of any and all left-leaning manifestations of identity politics. Another reminder that labels can suck.

'I'm not as upset as some early gay activists about the development of a more conservative queer attitude,' he says. 'As more and more lesbians and gays come out, the more they're going to be like the majority of the people in the country in which they live. Personally, I regret that there are so many high-profile gay Liberal members of parliament, but I think that's also just a reflection of reality. You may well be queer in your sexuality – it doesn't mean you're queer in your politics.'

O O O

'I want to live in a society that's diverse,' Andrea Goldsmith says. 'I'm Jewish. Sexually, I slide. I certainly don't fit into the standard lesbian category, and I don't fit into the heterosexual category either. I'm very happy sliding, and I've always known this. I come from a left-wing family and I have never, ever veered from that, so I have always welcomed diversity.'

There's a 'but' coming, you can probably sense it, and it has to do with the LGBTQIA+ spread.

'I think the intention of the alphabet stew is quite well-meaning,' she says. 'People are trying to be inclusive, but in doing so they're actually emulsifying our differences, and that's not diversity. The heterosexuals are in one group all by themselves, and all the non-hets are smooshed together. Seems to rather privilege the heterosexuals ...'

Even if one or more of the letters – roughly speaking – fits, they're rarely perfect. 'I for one do not want to define myself in terms of a single dimension. I would like to think that not just me but all of us are a little more complex than that.'

'Lesbian author' is not how Andrea would ever refer to herself, but others regularly do. 'It really, really shits me off,' she says. 'Someone helped me set up a Wikipedia page a long time ago and then I just left it. When I had a look a few years later, somebody had edited it to say "lesbian" in big letters. Everybody knows about my relationship with Dot, and I'm really happy about that, but I don't want to be locked into any corner.'

As with Dennis, 'queer' is Andrea's preferred nomenclature. 'I've always liked the idea of queer. It says "non-normative" and that suits me very well. And I can be queer for many reasons, only one of which might be my sexuality. I'm happy being a queer Jew. I'm *really* happy being a queer Australian – I certainly don't want to be a mainstream Australian like Scott Morrison, thank you very much.'

○○○

For Christos Tsiolkas, 'queer' evokes happy memories.

'I used to work at RMIT and knew the people who were doing the newspaper there,' he says. 'This would have been in 1988, the bicentenary year. I'd written an article on house music because I loved it and what it meant, and I remember having a discussion with the other people on the paper about the word "queer".

'What was lovely about it was, it didn't just mean Rob who was gay – it meant Julie, who was a strong feminist and a supporter of the queer people in her life. It felt like we could accomplish something.'

Like house music, he says, 'queer' was synonymous with pleasure. 'There was so much grimness at the time with AIDS and nuclear disarmament, with Reagan and Thatcher. And suddenly there was this explosive, happy moment, and "queer" was in that mix. It felt like it was part of a political moment – that it was angry but also fun.'

Prior to that time, he 'liked the provocation of throwing the word "poofter" into conversation. I remember thinking "gay" was this middle-class, safe word. I also used "homosexual" a lot because I wanted to put the sex back into the identity.'

'Queer' also fit well with his lifelong 'resistance to separatist politics'.

'When I was a young lad there was a lot of "gay only" or "women only" or "black only". I understand the animus of those politics, but because race, migration and class were so informative to my own politics, I felt that sexuality in isolation wasn't enough for me to make sense of myself.'

○○○

A side effect of writing books with characters from a sexual minority is that, like it or not, you'll probably be asked to speak about that minority position, often to the exlusion of the wider complexities and craft of your work.

'You end up on panel after panel that's the "LGBT+ diversity panel",' Holden Sheppard says. 'You know: *We've got three people here who are one of those letters.* And it's fine. I like that we're doing that. I like that my books have contributed to that conversation because it's an important conversation to be having. But sometimes you get there and you're thinking, "Just put me on a panel as an author who wrote a book that used language nicely or made you feel something ..." The diversity thing seems to obscure every other element of who you are.'

Three months have passed between my initial Instagram message to Holden to ask if I could interview him and the actual interview, but I remember very clearly how reticent – maybe even suspicious – he was to commit, and how tightly that was bound up in his understandable wariness of being labelled.

'I've never been comfortable with lumping myself into a really rigid category,' he says. 'So even when I came out, I was like "I'm homosexual, I'm same-sex attracted". I didn't really like the word 'gay' for me even, but then I was like, "No, I'm a gay man, I'll go with that".

'I remember one newspaper called my novel *Invisible Boys* a gay book, and I was like, "Yeah, fair call, it is". But then some people were like, "That's offensive. How dare a media outlet call you gay? You're LGBT-plus, you're queer, you're ..."

'But actually, I don't like the word "queer". I don't like the connotations of it. I don't like the sound of it. I don't like the denotative meaning of it even. I'm not LGBTQIA+ – I'm just the one letter. Lumping us all together is maybe helpful from a political lobbying or policy formation point of view where you're like, "Cool, here's all these weirdos, chuck them in together" – because that's effectively what they're saying. It reifies straight cisgender as the norm because "queer" means "strange", even if we reclaim it. It's never felt strange to me to be attracted to men – it feels natural and nice.

'I can't be a poster boy for LGBTQIA+ because I can't stand for all the letters that don't necessarily want the same things a homosexual man does. It's a really odd rubric.'

Expecting someone to be the spokesperson for even one letter, or any other identity, is a tall order. In interviews for *Poly*, I found myself trying to find lowest-common-denominator answers for lowest-common-denominator questions. If you're monogamous, try coming up with some on-the-spot answers to the following questions, in which I've swapped polyamory for monogamy:

Why do people go into monogamy?

Is being monogamous difficult?

What are the best and worst bits of being monogamous?

Is monogamy always ethical?

Other than being nonmonogamous, the only thing I've noticed all the nonmonogamous people I've met have in common, at least at the time of meeting them, is a pulse. My initial impressions of who they are come from things like their accent, clothes, hairstyle, smell, gait, hand gestures, sense of humour and personality.

At a deeper level, if we ever get there, my impressions – and sympathies – are informed by their political leanings, how they treat waiting staff, their trustworthiness, their attentiveness, how they talk about money and their family and friends, whether they turn up on time (and if/how they apologise when they don't).

Unless I'm sleeping with them, which is statistically unlikely, the mark of who someone is for me has very little – if anything – to do with their romantic or sexual preferences.

'I think we're on the same page there,' Holden says. 'I'm right-handed and whatever height and weight, and I happen to be homosexual, but they're just traits. They don't necessarily tell you who I am or if we'll like each other. There are plenty of individual LGBT people I can't stand because they're just really awful people.

'That doesn't mean I hate the letters or don't also know lots of LGBT people who are great – it just means I didn't like those particular people. There are also loads of straight cisgender people where I'm like, "fuck you, you're really horrible". Humans are humans. I feel very odd when the labels become the main thing about a person.'

OOO

'I tend not to introduce myself as nonmonogamous or polyamorous anymore,' Jinghua Qian says. 'I used to, but about 12 years ago I got a bit more involved in the poly communities through PolyVic and other organisations in Melbourne.'

Ey didn't enjoy those meet-ups. 'I was in my early twenties. A lot of the people were older and married – not necessarily heterosexual but usually a man–woman marriage, and often with kids. Lots of them, especially the older women I met, were perfectly lovely, and sometimes really interesting, but it just felt like there was nothing there for me. Their concerns were often around how they would describe their relationship to their friends and I was like, "I have none of these concerns". To me, it felt like talking to people who were becoming Mormons or something – I just couldn't relate.

'A lot of it was also the practical stuff of people's open relationships, so I was like, "OK, so this is more of a support group for a particular set of circumstances". It felt like people got really obsessed with the technical aspect of labelling and defining things. They seemed overly concerned with creating and using the language.'

○○○

Despite now identifying – and being identified – as non-binary, Ellen van Neerven knows the shortcomings of the terminology.

'I don't necessarily feel like I fit any sort of label,' they say, 'whether that's "non-binary" or "genderqueer", or anything else.'

There's a 'colonial gender binary' in Australia dating back to European arrival and dispossession, they say.

'When you read the way people were described in early settler reports, it was violently through the lens of gender. Settlers would only describe people they deemed to be women as inferior to how they thought white women should be, and only ever as sexual objects. They looked at figures they deemed to be male as symbols of fertility, and only in comparison to white males.

'There's a lot of violent history in the way Aboriginal people have been treated through a gender binary that was really only set up to compare and to qualify. In my limited understanding, gender identity here in so-called Australia was and is a lot more complicated, fluid and dynamic than what was written down and enforced when Europeans came here.

'People often talk about Western queer people appropriating non-Western ideas of gender fluidity and having more than two genders. All of that stuff was already there in so many different countries, and now white queers really love it. Whereas I think a lot of us that come from colonised peoples are still having to deal with homophobia and transphobia in our own communities following the imposition of religion on our communities – that's really a lot to unpack.

'There are lots of trans people that may not even identify as such because it doesn't fit with their cultural identity – they're already there without having to say those words.

'People are very quick to put those labels on you, which in some ways can be really good for a younger generation, or indeed an older generation, who are looking for representation and permission to be themselves, but in other ways it can be a little bit too much. You know, "non-binary, queer, Aboriginal ..." More and more things get added to how people want to describe you. In some ways it's accurate, but it's also just pointing out what's makes me different to your average dude.'

○ ○ ○

Such thoughts surely chime with Dr Arlie Alizzi, who wrote in his 2017 paper *Becoming-with and together: Indigenous transgender and transcultural practices*, that Indigenous trans people 'struggle to understand our gendered and sexual identities in relation to colonialism, to our relationships with religion, and our place within the queer community at large'.[41]

'When I wrote that, there was a discussion going on in Australia about a statistics-gathering project from the United States,' Arlie says. 'It was about counting the deaths by murder of trans people, and there was an attempt to make the project more global. But we have this absolute knowledge gap in the statistics when it comes to looking at how many transgender Aboriginal people have died each year in Australia. I think, at the time, they identified maybe three or four names.

'So there was this sense of queer and trans white people in the south-eastern states of Australia having no idea what's going on in Aboriginal Australia but being able to quote with confidence the trans politics of elsewhere.'

In that same paper, Arlie wrote about Indigenous queer and trans scholarship that links 'the formation of LGBTI identities in settler states with the establishment of settler colonial sovereignties and Indigenous dispossession, [while] identifying the colonising effect the settlercolonial LGBTI community has on Indigenous peoples.'

What does this mean, and what does it look like in practice? 'In the Anglosphere, in queer and trans Australia, there are norms around what it means to identify as trans that are not observed in Aboriginal communities all the time, or as consistently,' Arlie says. 'There are different words, different rules, different social norms. There's less fixation on identity as being attached to certain labels, so those labels can sometimes be very hard to comprehend.

'At a certain point in my involvement with the trans community in Melbourne, people would debate whether or not it was OK to use the word "transman" as opposed to putting a space between "trans" and "man". There was a fixation on the minutiae of the spelling that was deemed to be really offensive when people got it wrong.

'I didn't see that taking place in the Aboriginal community I was part of at the time, or not in the same way. There was a lot of mistranslation going on that really bothered me, and a lot of that was being informed by queer discourse from the United States. Theories can become another form of hierarchy and power exchange, of territory-marking in the community.'

Labels can be helpful, Arlie says, 'when they have utility. That's what they're for – they're just tools, especially identity words. You can't get caught up in whether or not you spell "transgender" a certain way and expecting everyone to know all the different layers of meaning. What use is that to you, especially when it comes to being able to organise as a community around it?

'Labels can't describe you, and you shouldn't seek recognition from them either, necessarily.'

Some of Arlie's thinking on the subject is informed by the American writer and founder of the Lesbian Herstory Archives, Joan Nestle, who lives in Australia and is a long-term patron of the Australian Gay and Lesbian Archives. 'In the last 20 or so years, Joan has written about how language has changed in the course of her writing career,' Arlie says. 'She said to me a while ago when we chatted that, when queer people get attached to notions like "butch" and "fem" and use them to exclude one another, they're replicating the behaviour of border police. I took a lot of instruction from that because, again, it raised the question of what these words are for. Why have the labels if we're not going to be able to make use of them?

'I guess for Aboriginal Australians it's tied in with the idea of the possessive [Anglo] culture. It's a culture about territory and taking and protecting and guarding what you have. It's not necessarily about sharing or being a community-minded person.

'Aboriginal people use those kinds of words with a lot more attention to personhood and connection to land. It's about people's wellbeing, rather than whether or not a word is OK for you to use.'

○ ○ ○

Using labels to describe yourself and having others use them to describe you are, of course, very different things, whether or not the labels you're employing are the same. A 2017 ABC article with the headline 'Meet Omar Sakr: Australia's queer Arab poet'[42] contains the preface to Omar's debut poetry collection, *These Wild Houses*, in which he writes:

> Now you are about to read the poetry of an Arab Australian, which is a rare thing when it shouldn't be. Now you are about to read the work of a queer Arab Australian, which is a rare thing when it shouldn't be. Now you are about to read the life of a queer Muslim Arab Australian from Western Sydney, from a broke and broken family — not rare, but it should be.[43]

When I first read this, I couldn't help thinking of the childhood memory game *I Went to the Shops*, in which each new person on their turn has to add another item that they got from the shops after accurately recounting the ever-expanding list of items that went before.

But in Omar's case each identifier comes loaded with more than the weight of groceries.

'It's not so much a question of self-assurance as it is a reflection of my lived experience and a certain amount of hopelessness,' he says. 'I have been made to reckon with my Arabness, my Turkishness, my Australianness, my Muslimness, and my queerness, or lack thereof, throughout my life.'

Leaning into those labels is partly about wrestling back ownership but also a means of exposing them, and the way they're often deployed, as problematic.

'One of the key outcomes of being constantly demeaned, dismissed and disadvantaged on the basis of your identity is that it diminishes your capacity to imagine an alternative way of living,' he says. 'The obsession with categorisation, with labels, and most of all with identity-based differences, is embedded in this imperialist white colonial society. It's posited now as coming from the "left" but this is nonsense.

'If there weren't material consequences for being anything other than a straight white cis man, we would not be stuck in this farcical discourse, which is not actually discourse as much as it is an abusive domineering relationship wherein one side refuses any attempts made at levelling the playing field.'

○ ○ ○

If our sexual – and therefore broader – identity is based on the gender of the people we're attracted to, feeling little or no sexual attraction to anyone complicates matters. In her 2018 article for *Archer* about coming out as asexual, author Gabrielle Ryan wrote:

> What does it mean to identify as something that is essentially an absence?

This is what I am thinking about, seven years into a happy straight-passing relationship with a cis-het man. It would be easy to continue in this relationship without coming out: just go on, not having sex, but not having to be seen as a sexual being by others because I am already 'taken'. It is the perfect cover; what goes on inside our bedroom is no-one else's business. But I'm uncomfortable when people assume I'm straight. I don't feel straight.[44]

Without naming names, a couple of the people I interviewed for this book raised their eyebrows at the mere mention of asexuality, with one going as far as to say it wasn't a real thing – a dismissal that's been levelled at most if not all letters in the LGBTQIA+ abbreviation at various and continuing points. Asexuality can be defined to some degree in opposition to 'allosexuals' (people who experience sexual attraction to others). For an asexual person, the sex drive may (or may not) be there; it could be very strong, very weak or somewhere in between – it's just not directed at you, me, or anyone else (or, at least, not consistently).

'Asexuality is a spectrum,' Gabrielle says. 'It's important to realise it's not one thing, that people are at different places on that spectrum, and that it can change at different points in your life. Just because you feel sexual attraction at certain times doesn't mean you're not asexual. In my case, I didn't have a lightning-bolt moment – it was a gradual realisation.'

Gabrielle's *Archer* article functioned as her public coming-out. 'I hadn't identified myself as asexual to very many people at the time,' she remembers. 'I'd not even talked specifically to my partner about it. We'd discussed the fact we didn't see it as a failure that we weren't having sex but without ever using the word. It wasn't really until I wrote the article that I had to put some language around it and artic-ulate what it meant for me.'

While the term felt accurate and useful, there was still the question of how – and why – to come out. 'It doesn't necessarily change who you're going to bring home for Christmas,' she says. 'But it was important for me because I'd never felt I was straight, even though I was in this straight-passing relationship. It felt really right to identify as asexual and to have that affinity with my queer identity.'

The decision, she says, settled some questions and raised others. 'It helps me make sense of the things I've done in my life and why certain times were difficult but it's not comparable to someone who has real gender or body dysmorphia. It's not like being a cisgender lesbian or gay man who's been bullied their whole life and had an awful time coming out to their parents. There are very different experiences contained within the LGBTQIA+ letters.

'Even though asexuality is hugely questioning and rejecting of the norm in the same way those other letters are, there's also … I don't know if it's an internalised phobia, but I feel that I'm not on the same platform as lots of those people who didn't even have the choice to pass as straight.'

Lest we think gender and sexuality labels can be a source of consternation only for LGBTQIA+ people, Gabrielle offers an illustrative – and endearing – account of her partner's reaction to her *Archer* article.

'I guess I felt it was a very private thing when I wrote it, even though I was writing it to be published,' she says. 'I didn't actually think about what it might have meant for him.

'Quite a while later, he told me he felt as if I'd outed him, which initially surprised me, but of course it had an impact. I'd written that I was in a relationship with a "cis-het man" and he didn't know what that meant because he's not in a world where that kind of language is used very often. When we looked it up, he was like, "Ah, yeah, OK, I think that's what I am". Now he uses that terminology all the time, so we've got to a good place with it.'

7
Taxonomy for three, please!

You don't have to go far to find guidebooks on nonmonogamy. They've become their own mini-genre, from bestsellers – *The Ethical Slut* – to evocative, seemingly catch-all titles such as *What Love Is: And What It Could Be*. Much like *How To Be Gay* or *The Lesbian Handbook*, they're directed at those already in – or realising they maybe should be in – the trenches.

They tend to be American in origin and sensibility, pushing back on a prevailing 'mononormative' culture while offering instruction (or were they rules?) on the ethical bits of ethical nonmonogamy. Generally, they're about as sexy as a slipped disc. Take this case study from what many refer to as the 'polyamory bible', *More Than Two*:

> For two years, they used [a spreadsheet] to track the time they spent together: what scheduled time they missed, what unscheduled time they added. It tracked hours spent and lost, and whether Joseph spent time with Audrey and Jasmine individually or together as family time. Time on the phone was logged in its own category ...[45]

You get the gist.

I don't want to knock those books. They've provided many people, myself included, with frameworks and terminology that can be adopted, modified or rejected – ways to at least start making sense of what might otherwise remain an atomised and largely directionless experience. But they do underscore how the American viewpoint (or many millions of viewpoints trending towards the top of the great American bell curve) colours so much of what and how we expect things to be.

Unless you've been in the Australian version, your mental image of a courtroom probably comes from American TV. Objection? Overruled! If you watch porn, it's probably been built on a bedrock of American puritanism, its risqué nature more in tune with someone from Milwaukee than Mallacoota. If you wear a commercial fragrance, its base note will likely be that baby-powder smell that appeals to American noses. Eat a burger, hold a gun, picture someone on a horse, the list goes on ...

The dissonance comes not from seeing how Americans do things differently to us but from realising we do things differently to Americans, and the fact that ... maybe that's OK. It's a big world. Polyandrists in Tibet – where women don't necessarily know the biological fathers of their children and all spouses are treated equally – probably aren't rushing out to buy *The Smart Girl's Guide to Polyamory*.

Are those women nonmonogamous? Yes. Are we? Yes! No! Maybe! Having multiple partners is automatically respectable only if we're talking about a legal firm. One plus one plus one is easier in maths than life.

Our views on nonmonogamy are stitched into too many interlinking fabrics to unpick – a personal under-sheet stuck to a familial top sheet sewn into a socioreligious blanket that's bound to a polyphonic global doona. Little wonder inconsistency is the only constant.

The rich 'take lovers' or 'keep mistresses' while the rest of us 'have affairs'. Writers and artists are in 'bohemian' open relationships while Tracy from the servo is a 'slut'.

The developing taxonomy of ethical nonmonogamy is an attempt to normalise (even at the cost of neutering) the discussion. And it kind of works, sometimes. The 'ethical' prefix is a decent flotation aid but there's only so far it can lift the dead weight of 'non' in nonmonogamous, the sense that, if not wrong, nonmonogamy is nominally nonsensical – or worse.

'Women who are polyamorous are basically saying "sexual pleasure is important to me",' Rochelle Siemienowicz says. 'I mean, you can be asexual and poly, of course, but most polyamorous women are interested in having sex with more than one person.

'That's still a pretty radical thing to say – not only that you might be having a number of Tinder dates to try and find *the one* but that you'll continue to have lots of partners.

'One of the most subversive things about polyamory is that you can look your partner full in the face and say, "I really love you, and I want to fuck someone else". And not just that but, "I want to be able to fall in love with that other person too. I want to form a connection with them that may involve its own commitments and obligations that'll affect my commitments and obligations to you".'

O O O

'Is there a part of it that's exciting?' Filip Vukašin asks.

By 'it', he means being actively polyamorous in an ostensibly monogamous society, with the heady brew of nerves and latent judgement that entails.

'Me and Matt have had this conversation in relation to the shift in culture around gay relationships and acceptance,' he says. 'When it was secret and forbidden, it was more exciting. When we went to Serbia, where my family is from, and which is open-ish but still relatively conservative, we didn't hold hands on the street or show any affection – we were just two mates. And then you go into a lift and the door closes and you pash each other – you're doing something that you're not allowed to do, and it's a bit dangerous but nice as well. Have you felt that with polyamory?'

I'm not sure how to respond at the time but, on thinking about it since, I suppose my honest answer is: not really. Having only had one partner outside of my marriage has felt in some ways like a double serving of heterosexual monogamy – it's almost as if I'm doing twice as much to uphold traditionally accepted relationship structures as my straight monogamous friends.

But I get Filip's point. In all the religiously informed suppression of people, the codification of what is and isn't allowed, the finger-wagging of the unquestioningly self-righteous; in all the heartache and grief, all the many ways in which we punish and trample on others and ourselves despite the fact most of us are fundamentally good and living overwhelmingly law-abiding lives, it's easy to forget that transgression is sexy. The crunch and slurp of Eve biting into the forbidden fruit in the Garden of Eden, Adam's irrepressible temptation to follow suit, their lips glistening as the juice runs down their chins and onto their naked torsos ... I mean, it's meant to be hot, right?

For those of us riddled with original sin – which in Christian-heritage cultures is the majority of us – few experiences compare to the visceral thrill of failing, just momentarily, to keep our libidos in check. In the definitely-not-sex-related words of Ralph from the 2012 kids film *Wreck-it-Ralph*, during a group therapy session with other arcade game villains: 'I'm bad, and that's good. I will never be good, and that's not bad. There's no-one I'd rather be than me.'[46]

The letting-off of steam that comes from hopping temporarily over the propriety fault line was well understood by rulers in ancient Rome. Bread, circuses and bacchanalian behaviour were permitted as a means of political control, with the understanding that those privileges could and would be yanked away when the authorities said so.

Which is the crux of it, really, and the reason it feels scary to veer from our appointed lanes. Adam and Eve were evicted from Paradise.

In ancient Rome, civic retribution for transgressive behaviour could be as swift and capricious as the gods it was designed to appease. Have your fun, in other words, but remember: it always comes at a cost.

○ ○ ○

Dr Jessica Kean is a Lecturer in the Department of Gender and Cultural Studies at the University of Sydney, whose research interests include monogamy, nonmonogamy and queer theory. As with Roz Bellamy, she's ridden more than one coming-out rodeo.

'I came out as queer quite young,' she says. 'That wasn't completely without difficulty, but it came good really quickly. Most people knew which side of that they wanted to be on and got themselves around to it pretty quickly (if they weren't already there). Before long I was surrounded by queer folk and openly celebratory allies.

'Later, when I was a young adult, I was in a thruple that was significant enough in my life that I decided to come out about it too. And that was a totally different ballgame – I really wasn't expecting it.

'A couple of people even came around to my house as soon as they heard, full of concern, almost like an intervention. They were worried that someone was getting hurt, although they weren't quite sure who, and they wanted to have big, serious conversations about it.

'Those people became supportive in the end, but it felt like a very conditional kind of support, full of anxiety and concern.'

I ask Jessica about the ways monogamy is ingrained not just in society but in law – which she's happy to speak about with the caveat that she's a researcher, not a lawyer. 'The most obvious part of the law that enshrines monogamy is marriage,' she says. 'Through the whole same-sex marriage debate and postal vote there was this sense of trying to protect monogamy – this idea that "We're good monogamous citizens, just like you, therefore give us marriage". That tone was there throughout the whole thing. And on the flipside, there were the conservatives, who were saying, "The queers have their strange relationships and if you allow them to marry, they might undermine marriage with their nonmonogamy. If we allow two gay men to marry each other, are we going to have to allow five gay men to marry each other?"'

The official understanding of what marriages *should* look like is, in practice, a set of legal principles and the shifting social attitudes that inform and transform them. Most obviously, marriages, we know, are between two, and only two, individuals – a couple. But what, exactly, do we mean by 'couple'?

The laws around de facto relationships offer some clues, Jessica says. There are differences in interpretation across Australia's states and territories, but a common understanding is that a de facto couple is two people, whether same sex or opposite sex, who have lived together as a couple without separation for two years. Provided that's the case – and you're not married to each other or related by family – you have certain rights regarding property settlement, child maintenance and separation under Australia's Family Law Act.

'Most of us become de facto without necessarily thinking about it,' Jessica says. 'But when you see people having fights about whether they're de facto in courts and tribunals, you get these hilarious moments where very serious lawyerly people are trying to put down in concrete terms whether or not this couple is a de facto couple, and why. They'll make all of these statements about what it means to be a couple – and monogamy often features in those. There have been cases where people have been declared not a couple for Centrelink payments, say, based on the fact they weren't monogamous.'

Among the factors brought to bear are the length of the relationship, the level and type of financial dependency, the sexual nature and – most nebulously – public reputation of the relationship.

'Basically, you can be de facto and nonmonogamous but it's dicey terri-tory,' Jessica says. 'If you and your partner are both openly like, "Hey, we're sleeping with other people," the courts may question whether you're a couple. But, funnily, if either party is cheating without the other person's knowledge, that wouldn't discount them from being classified as de facto.'

'There's also the insistence on the importance of cohabitation – so living apart would traditionally make it difficult, if not impossible, to be classified as de facto.'

The trend in the last couple of decades, driven by iterative legislative changes (including recognising same-sex couples as de facto in 2009), has removed some – but not all – of the burden of proving the 'mar-riage-like' nature of de facto relationships.

'A married couple can actually look like anything,' Jessica says. 'You can live in different countries, you can live nonmonogamously, and you'll still be married. If you're in a de facto couple and you don't look the way a court thinks a married couple should look, there's still the chance you'll no longer be considered to be in a de facto relationship.'

OOO

Dennis Altman thinks we live in a couple culture. 'The couple is reinforced constantly, in all sorts of ways,' he says. 'Advertising now increasingly likes to show bi-racial couples, same-sex couples, but there's still this very strong emphasis on the couple.

'The basic assumption in gay male relationships is that people are not going to be monogamous. Because of that, there's a much greater acceptance that monogamy is probably something that is hard to attain.

'That's not the same as polyamory, which implies the possibility of having several serious emotional relationships. Although there are plenty of examples of both homosexual and heterosexual couples who do expand, where a threesome or foursome might develop, or both partners have other partners. I think that's probably more widely practised than we know because there's such pressure to maintain this myth of the perfect coupling.

'In same-sex or opposite-sex weddings there's still a large echo of the old Christian belief that marriage is for life – but that doesn't necessarily mean anything more than "you will only have sex with this other person until one or the other of you drops dead". How terrible.'

○ ○ ○

'We're brought up with the notion that monogamy is normal and natural,' Andrea Goldsmith says. 'But during the '70s, nonmonogamy among people on the left was absolutely the thing. And not only that – we weren't allowed to be jealous either.'

Oof. Yes. Jealousy.

Ouch.

According to a post on the polyamory blog *More Than Two*, dealing effectively with jealousy involves some self-talk, like the following:

> I know that I am feeling jealous. I know that the jealousy is brought about by some other emotion – some emotion that is triggered by the action that makes me jealous. I need to figure out what that other emotion is, and I need to figure out why that action triggers that emotion.[47]

In a piece for Guardian Australia in 2020, meanwhile, I wrote that:

> In my case, jealousy has triggered everything from spontaneously smashing the tiles on my bathroom wall with my fist to panic attacks that haven't just given the impression I'm dying – I've been

convinced I really am dying, my lungs collapsing under the heavy existential fear that I'm going to be left alone, subbed out for someone fitter, happier, more productive.[48]

While it's nice to daydream about a version of myself that aligns better with the best practice around jealousy, I take consolation from the fact that others also find it hard.

'I confess to you that there were many nights I sat outside the house of somebody that I was madly in love with, watching what they were doing with someone they were madly in love with,' Andrea says. 'From a personal point of view, I find nonmonogamy that is ongoing difficult, whether that involves two couples or three people.

'What I absolutely don't find difficult is the notion of nonmonogamy where you have a primary person and that relationship is central, and you go to a literary festival and have a little one-night stand or a long weekend and come home again. I've never had a problem with that.'

○ ○ ○

Christos Tsiolkas and his partner Wayne have been together for nearly four decades, their relationship starting when Christos was 19. 'I didn't think of having sex with anyone else at the start,' he says. 'Because it was that honeymoon period. But then a type of radicalisation began for both of us, where part of being queer was about leading unorthodox sexual lives. From there, for the next seven or eight years of the relationship, we were nonmonogamous, which meant hurting each other because it was really about falling in love with other people.'

There was – maybe unavoidably – conflict. 'I had a really loving friendship and sexual relationship with a wonderful man, an Australian writer called Sasha Soldatow, who was a generation older than we were.

'Wayne and I were living in Collingwood and Sasha, who lived in Sydney, came and lived with us. It was a tumultuous period. Sasha was of that generation that had come through gay liberation. He'd also come through an anarchist politics that I deeply respected back then, and still do now. But I was always deeply aware of certain commitments that come from living those politics that I wasn't prepared to make, and I think that was largely around family.'

Christos and Wayne left Melbourne and went their separate ways for a year – which allowed some time for reassessing their relationship and 'drying out' from various addictions. When they reunited, they discussed monogamy.

'The real scarring was probably about the people we were having other relationships with, because they got hurt in the fallout,' Christos says. 'When it came to us, Wayne articulated it really well: if we were going to get back together, we were committing to the future being the both of us, no longer the individual "I". We made a decision to be emotionally monogamous, but realising that sex can still happen.

'We decided that what we would do, in those instances, was keep it anonymous – you know, sex clubs, doing it with strangers. There have been hiccups along the way but we've both pretty much maintained that.

'Now we're at an age where we're just really into each other, which is really nice.'

○ ○ ○

In *The Dangerous Bride*, Lee Kofman writes that, since meeting her husband Daryl, she has given up on certain relationship dreams and committed to monogamy:

'True love certainly makes fidelity easier. But I believe that if I hadn't lived messily before I met Daryl, hadn't wrestled with that mess, I'd most likely not have managed to preserve our love [...] Monogamy now feels like a choice I've made, rather than an imperative.'[49]

But that was in 2014 – is she still happy living monogamously now?

'Look, it's a compromise,' she says. 'I fell in love with someone who was into monogamy and just went with that. But of course there's a cost, and I feel a certain part of me is not alive. It's worth it for me, but it's not easy.'

'I feel it's part of who I am to be nonmonogamous. I'm a very greedy person. I've had lots of different so-called careers or professions, I speak a few languages, I change my hair colour every so often, I change my writing styles and genres.

'I'm also very aware of my own mortality because as a child I had open-heart surgery and knew from a very young age that I could die. I always want to do a lot and I think it's the same for me when it comes to my love life. It's hard for me to be content with just one relationship.'

I'm interested to know whether nonmonogamy is a sexual orientation or a lifestyle choice, but I'm also fairly confident there's no one answer. For some people, it's very much who they are, for others, it's who they sometimes are, or would sometimes or always like to be, for others ... I don't know. Does it matter? Yes, it does.

In an article for *Psychology Today* in 2016, author and researcher Elisabeth A. Sheff wrote that:

> Legally, polyamory is not considered a sexual orientation in the United States (or anywhere else, to my knowledge) and so is not eligible for protected status under statutes that protect people from employment and housing discrimination based on sex, sexuality, or gender.

She reminds us that 'sexual orientation' is a nineteenth-century construct that relies on the biological sex of our desired partners to sort us into our respective homo, hetero and bi baskets. But:

> Such a simplistic view of sexuality fails to adequately encompass the enormous range of sexual and gender diversity that exists today. Contemporary sexual orientation includes a far wider array of factors, including (but not limited to): type of sex, presence or absence of desire for sex and relational configuration.[50]

○ ○ ○

In his essay *Building a Household,* published in the book *Queerstories* in 2018, Simon Copland writes about the same-old-same-old nature of his domestic life – the weekly shop, doing the dishes, mopping the floor – and the not-so-typical nature of what Sheff would call his relational configuration:

> Instead of living with my one 'soulmate', I live with my two partners: James and Martyn. While James and Martyn are good friends they are not romantically attached. So, in this household of ours, I decide which room I'll sleep in on a nightly basis. While we spend a lot of time doing things as a trio, I often need to find ways to spend time separately with each of them, making sure we make space to be both couples, and an amazing threesome.[51]

Both of us look, feel and sound groggy on Zoom the day we chat – one of Simon's partners is in bed with Covid, and my eldest son also has it. I feel like I probably have it too but keep testing negative. It's probably fine, then, that we start by sharing negative emotions – particularly old mate jealousy.

'The thing I hear most is, "I couldn't do that because I'd get too jealous",' Simon says. 'It's really interesting how jealousy is seen as an emotion that can't be dealt with or managed – that people don't ask themselves *Why am I so jealous? What's going on? Why is this impacting me so much? What kind of experiences am I stopping myself and my part-ner from enjoying?'*

I want to agree, and do, theoretically, but I also shudder at how diffi-cult it can be in practice. Although practice helps.

The first time I was at home knowing Jess was with someone else overnight was probably equal parts exciting and hive-inducing. But as the months went on, it really depended on the person. If someone seemed cooler than me (and frankly, that's not hard), it could be a struggle. If they were into books, music and visual art – well, pass them over here, honey, I'll sleep with them too.

'The relationships where I see jealousy most prominently are monoga-mous,' Simon says. 'This plays out a lot in TV shows and movies, where a character is friendly with someone of the opposite sex. I remember watching an episode of *Sex and the City* where Carrie's with Big and gets really offended by him checking out other women. As if, you know, because he's with her, he suddenly doesn't find anyone attrac-tive anymore. It's a trope within monogamous relationships. Because monogamy papers over any other relationships or desires, jealousy is taken as a sign something is inherently wrong rather than part of living.'

Like me, Simon believes 'people should be able to enter whatever relationship they want, and that we should be able to figure out legal systems that accept that'.

The legal side came to the fore in 2021 when he and his partners bought a property. 'Buying the house itself actually wasn't that dif-ficult,' he says. 'Multiples buy houses all the time – so we now own a third of the house each. But we did have to have complex conversa-tions about what happens if I break up with one of my partners and that person wants to leave, and how we negotiate that.

'Does all of his share go to me? Or does it split to both, to the other, to all of us equally? And then what happens if one of us dies? The legal system is certainly not set up to deal with that. We spoke to a lawyer who said we'd all need individual representation and that it would cost us a fortune. So we've written down our own agreement that's not legally binding but would hopefully hold some sort of emotional force.'

Do people – and therefore legislators – just find it hard to envisage three, four or more people being committed to each other romantically? In my case, I've been told more than once by friends and extended family members to keep my relationship status under wraps from someone else known to all of us who 'wouldn't understand' – which seems like a strange indictment of that other person's intelligence. We're not talking nanophysics – it's just love, and we're bombarded with that concept and reality constantly.

'You would never say to a parent, "How is it you can love both your children?"' Simon says. 'Or, "How do you manage to have more than one friend?" But when it comes to someone you're engaged with romantically, they're like, "How could you possibly have feelings for more than one person?"'

'We have this ability to love. You know, I love my family and I love my friends, and nobody would ever question that when I say it.'

'There was a period of having to tell people I was poly where it felt like a second coming out. People were worried I was breaking up with my longer-term partner or that there was something wrong. I think, being gay, you get used to those moments, you know, the first time you say "my boyfriend" – you're always on guard about that and having to negotiate a way forward.

'With polyamory, it's quite amusing how people suddenly feel the need to ask intimate questions they'd have never asked before, like: "Where do you sleep?"' People in monogamous relationships have different sleeping arrangements but people generally don't delve into those details with them.

'The other thing, particularly with gay men, is that they see it as being super-hot, as if we're having sex all the time and they can come and join in, so you have to explain that's not how it is. There are different levels of discussion required compared to just coming out and being gay.'

In his *Queerstories* essay, Simon writes about getting 'pushback' from gay men and lesbians – 'a group we did not expect' – when he started identifying publicly as polyamorous.

> One even told me that we have to restrict polyamory as it hurts children – spoken with the same confidence and lack of evidence as conservatives who say the same things about gay parents [...] In recent years the gay movement has rammed the idea that 'all love is equal' down everyone's throats [...] But the response to our relationships has shown me that this equality only extends to love that happens between two monogamous gays, behind the closed doors of a bedroom in a moderately sized apartment, with their sex now legitimised by the state.[52]

'To an extent, it was a shock,' he says. It was a particularly heightened time with the marriage equality campaign, but I remember having debates with people online who were using very similar language to the kind that used to be used against gay people. Gay men were targeted for being promiscuous and dirty, a danger to society, and now those same men were targeting poly people in that way.

'There was, and still is, a lot of what I call "respectability politics", where the way of presenting gay people as respectable is through the monogamous ideal, to show that we're just like the rest of society. You could see it in the imagery that was used in the marriage equality campaign – all those pictures of white, conventionally attractive monogamous couples, where the men were always wearing tuxedos and the women wore wedding dresses. The messaging was basically: *Give us this and we will behave and stop being those dirty gays you see us as.* It created a limiting politics around what relationships could look like and I think that's really quite disappointing.

'I'd hear things like, "Can you just not talk about nonmonogamy for now? We need to focus on marriage equality first and then we can talk about those other issues". And naturally, that hasn't happened.'

8
Let's not necessarily talk about sex

Remember when Christos Tsiolkas said he used to like describing himself as 'homosexual' for the emphasis it put on 'sex'? I've been thinking about that lately, and more broadly about the etiquette governing where and when it's deemed acceptable to talk about the peculiarities of our individual sex lives, the rule of thumb being: if you're in any way unsure, employ the old yeah-nah.

When a colleague asks how you're going, they probably don't want to hear about the amazing shag you had this morning; they're not inviting you to tell them you were masturbating for Australia until your snooze alarm went off for the third time and you huffily got out of bed.

Regardless of how important (or not) sex is to us, we mostly prefer to store our own experiences in the private and largely hidden filing cabinets of our lives, just one divider over from what came out of our bodies in the toilet. Which in some ways is a pity. A few years ago, an able-bodied cis male friend of mine asked me if I – like he – enjoyed sitting down on the toilet to urinate even when I didn't need to poo. I told him I preferred standing, even though I sometimes get performance anxiety in busy public urinals, but it was a moment of bonding all the same.

I think sex-positivity of the kind Christos was alluding to is rare – and even rarer the opportunities to talk candidly about our sex lives and their intricacies, whether that's with our friends, peers or the people we're having sex with. We're not exactly well-practised – unsurprisingly maybe, given at least half of us are steeped from a young age in what Chanel Contos of the advocacy group Teach Us Consent calls 'taught shame'.

In a 2023 article for Guardian Australia, Contos decried the 'purity culture' of sex education in Australian schools, with lessons 'that still frame sex as a shameful act for women and girls and places boys and men in the role of having to convince or hoodwink them'.

Consent – and therefore, ideally, the opportunity to talk openly about sexual wants and don't-wants – should be at the heart of sex education, Contos wrote. 'A recent survey in Australia found that 60% of students aged 14 to 18 are sexually active (defined by engaging in oral, vaginal or anal sex). If we are educating for the purpose of safety, then the central concern should not be whether students are engaging with sex at all, but rather whether they are practising consensual sex.'[53]

Ironically, while most of us are keeping schtum about our own sex lives and their associated issues, we're being bombarded with stylised versions of (or nods towards) sex on TV and radio; in books, cinema, magazines, porn, advertising and music; in stand-up comedy, theatre, pub gossip and (occasionally) friendly banter – an unendingly chaotic communiqué about what's right and wrong to lust after, take a stand against or even mention.

Holden Sheppard, who happily identifies as sex-positive, thinks there's now a 'virtuous version' of gay identity that airbrushes the sex out of sexuality. 'If you look at the gay stories that are getting published and selling well at the moment, they're actually terrifyingly and increasingly chaste – you know, where they'll kiss and the writer pans away. TV's going the other way and getting quite good in this space, but there are a lot of straight women writing successful male-male romances that are sexless and don't represent what most guys are like, gay or otherwise.

'I think an unfortunate by-product of our successful quest for more mainstream acceptance of gay people is that, for the last 40 years, we've increasingly created this space where we're saying "Don't talk about the sex – just remember that love is love". And that's fine, but it sometimes means we're imposing a version of shame onto the sex act. It's okay to be gay only if it's this squeaky-clean, family-friendly Disney version of what "gay" is.

'I've fucked so many guys who have a really safe, painfully wholesome gay thing going on in public and they're dirty as hell in private. It feels like so many guys are doing it in order to garner broader social acceptance.

'I don't do it: I'm not here to be gentrified for straight acceptance and I don't think that's the way forward. I'm open about who I am: an unabashedly horny, red-blooded homosexual male. I want us to find our way back to being ourselves without shame.'

Of course, if you're in any way squeamish or shy, it's probably for the best that a degree of prudishness rules the day. My first long-term partner – a Spanish woman with Portuguese and Japanese parents – once asked my paternal grandparents, in their seventies at the time, if they still had sex, and if not, why.

My grandma said they didn't and sounded pretty calm as she started talking about my grandad's erectile issues (I didn't see her face because I was looking at the floor, mortified). My grandad didn't reply, which made me think he was struggling too, but in reality he'd turned down his hearing aid, a trick he employed in company regularly and which only became apparent when my gran shouted – 'I'M JUST EXPLAINING WHY WE DON'T BONK ANYMORE' – to which he just said 'Oh, aye ...' and left it at that.

Wherever you sit on the shrinking violet scale, you're at a distinct advantage – one of many – if you're heterosexual. You might nod when someone asks if Colin over there is your boyfriend or says that you and Colleen look good together, and that's about as far as your hetero-confession needs to go. In chips terms, you're ready-salted, unlikely to cause offence or set hearts and minds racing. Any other flavour and you're going to have to make it known many times over in all sorts of situations, including those where lime and black pepper isn't to everyone's taste. Oh, you've never tried honey soy? You once knew an annoying caramelised onion? You'd prefer – present company excepted – that those smokey bacon chips kept themselves to themselves?

In clarifying for any number of mundane reasons that you're gay, lesbian, bi, pan or poly, you're opening yourself to a level of profiling and preconception that Hugo the hetero handyman rarely has to contend with.

'I can see how someone coming from a conservative perspective might think "my god, gay people are obsessed with sex and sexuality",' Filip Vukašin says. 'They might say things like: 'They have their Pride March – why don't we have a Straight March?" But the truth is I don't want to be obsessed with those things either – they're such a small part of me. The problem is that other, more conservative, people make a big deal about it and, whether you're gay or lesbian or any other sexuality, that can lead to you embracing those parts of your identity even more. It's as if you dig your heels in and those things define you even though they're only one aspect of you.'

○ ○ ○

If you *are* having sex, another big concern is whether you're having *enough* of it. According to a 2019 article on *The Conversation*:

> Australians report having sex once or twice a week, on average. For Brits, it's less than once a week, while Americans report having sex two to three times a week.[54]

After that, the question that follows for many people is whether they're having it for long enough, the best scientific answer to which is ... probably. A 2005 study of 500 heterosexual couples from the Netherlands, UK, Spain, Turkey and the US found that male–female penetrative sex typically lasted anywhere from 33 seconds to 44 minutes, the difference roughly between a YouTube ad and an episode of *Breaking Bad*.[55]

To put that in perspective, even if you're at the top end of the Australian sex norm, doing it a whopping two times weekly for nearly three quarters of an hour each time, that leaves about 99 per cent of the week that you're doing something else.

Though it's tempting to think of humans as runaway steam trains of androgens, estrogens and progestogens, driven – as evolutionary biologists would have it – by a do-or-die need to propagate the species, that's clearly not the case for everyone. Gay and lesbian sex doesn't produce babies, non-penetrative sex doesn't produce babies, and some of us have either no urge or a libido that exists without attaching itself to others.

'I don't know what sexual attraction feels like,' Gabrielle Ryan says.

We've been talking about the work of American author Angela Chen – who wrote the 2020 book *ACE: What Asexuality Reveals about Desire, Society and the Meaning of Sex* – and in particular the concept of compulsory sexuality, which Chen, in a 2020 interview for *them*, described this way:

> Compulsory sexuality is the idea that all normal people want and desire sex, that everyone has this baseline level of sexual desire. If you assume that everyone has that baseline, then when they say no for seemingly no reason, then it seems like they're being mean to you or they're being withholding or they are denying you something, right? [...] But the truth is not everyone has that baseline of sexual desire. And for many people they don't want to because they don't want to.[56]

That idea, and much of Chen's writing, resonates with Gabrielle. 'She writes about all the ways sexual relationships are seen as the pinnacle, and how other types are seen as lesser, even though they can be just as important and fulfilling. I found that to be really liberating.'

As an asexual cis woman in a monogamous long-term relationship, the nature of Gabrielle's interactions with people varies greatly. 'I'm definitely romantically monogamous but the absence of sexual attraction gives me the opportunity to explore platonic love more,' she says. 'I can fall a little bit in love with my friends but it's a "friend-love" that's different to what I feel for my partner.

'For allosexuals, the difference between platonic and romantic love tends to be sex or sexual attraction, but I think my asexuality shows me that's too simplistic.'

Gabrielle's journey, like most people's, hasn't been straightforward. As she explains in her 2018 *Archer* article, it's taken a lot of trial, error and confusion to reach her current point of relative peace:

> There were many one-night stands with men I met at pubs, men I impressed with my knowledge about sport and my ability to match them beer for beer, and who I never saw again. I had sex with them, but it was always going through the motions. I used sex as currency: it was the payment for the conversation, the belonging.[57]

'We all crave connection, and the expectation is often that sex is how you get that,' she says. 'But in those sorts of situations in the past, I'd always feel guilty in the morning after a one-night stand because the part I actually enjoyed was back at the pub having the great conversation.'

Removing sex from the menu opens up different courses of action, she says, whether that's with friends and acquaintances out in the world or at home, behind closed doors.

'It takes the pressure off me and, I think, my partner too,' she says. 'I've said to him before, 'If you ever feel like you need to have sex, we can talk about what that might mean, whether it's going to be with me or not. I don't want him to feel trapped in something he's not happy with. I've left that door open and we both have some agency in what this might look like and what it could be.'

Another pressure it alleviates is that of the 'unhappily sexless relationship', Gabrielle says, which rarely comes without a super serve of judgement and a side of self-loathing.

Ongoing romantic relationships are considered sexless, by most measures, when the couple in question is doing the wild thing fewer than ten times a year. Self-reporting studies suggest about 15 per cent of relationships dip below that waterline (usually because of the disinclination or inability of one of the partners to have sex) but in cultures in which virility and desirability are as vital to social mobility as a driving licence, underreporting seems likely.

Certainly, in a straw poll of my friends in long-term relationships, the 'fewer than ten times a year' tally applies to more than 15 per cent, particularly those in relationships involving childcare. Tales are common of sleeping on sofas, of tossing and turning on a mattress on the floor, of the much-talked-of 'lesbian bed death', whereby lesbian couples are thought to have (even) less sex than other people in long-term relationships ... It seems to be pretty common.

Going by the numbers, I've spent about 15 years of my adult life in a sexless relationship. In that same period, I immigrated to Australia, wrote books, helped start a successful website, raised two children, grieved family members, rode bikes many thousands of kilometres, became an Australian citizen, felt homesick for Scotland, and related – quietly and morosely – to much of what's available online about sexless relationships. In fact, if there are articles and testimonials on this topic I haven't read I'd be surprised. Many describe – though less eloquently – the red-hot frustration and plummeting self-esteem of the sort Rochelle Siemlenowicz conjures in her memoir *Fallen* when writing about the lack of sex in her first marriage:

> I felt the shame of it. And then the anger. As the months wore on, I raged and I screamed and I broke things. I threw our framed wedding photo against the kitchen wall and left Isaac to clean up the shards of glass [...] Often I locked myself in the bathroom, sitting in the shower recess, my head on my knees, until the water turned cold and Isaac was banging on the door to make sure I hadn't passed out or tried to slit my wrists.[58]

'Looking back on it now, I see that so much of my pain was caused by an expectation that marriage and sex would go together,' Rochelle says, 'and that physical intimacy was the ultimate verification of love. Being raised as a young woman in a religious culture that emphasised waiting for sex until marriage, I was devastated to find I was also waiting and longing for it afterwards. The rejection felt total.

'Women have been taught that men are sexually voracious, and that women must be the gatekeepers and moderators of this vital force. So when I realised I was the more desirous partner in my marriage, I felt like a complete freak. People told me I was "masculine" for wanting it so badly, so this emphasised the threat to my sense of self and my femininity. What was wrong with me?

'Thirty years later, and in supposedly more enlightened times, I still see Australian culture as incredibly impoverished when it comes to speaking of sex, desire, love and the real complexity and diversity of physical pleasure. As a publicly polyamorous woman and the writer of an explicit memoir, I'm still considered a freak in more conservative circles because I'm a woman who's admitted the central role of sexual desire in my happiness.'

In my own case, it's only in recent years that I've realised something else was happening to me that I was unaware of at the time – a gradual untethering of myself from my limbs, head and torso. As a married man with a young family, the thought of flirting with anyone outside of my marriage would have made me uncomfortable simply because that's not the kind of person I wanted to be. But the truth is, I didn't even think about flirting or expect anyone to flirt with me. I felt invisible. If I'd sat in my room and unwrapped the bandages there would have been nothing there, my transparency scaring the landlady and any other villagers peeking through the keyhole of my miserable lodgings. I'd crossed the world and had nobody that had ever known me – other than Jess – for anything other than the incorporeal being I'd become.

Writing about her own sexless marriage in *The Dangerous Bride*, Lee Kofman perfectly sums up this spectral reality:

> During my years with Noah, I'd sometimes forget I had a body or, rather, the kind of body that could be loved.[59]

'Those years were tough,' she says now, reflecting on that period of her life. 'It was as if I lost a particular part of myself – the sparkly, wild part. I was trying to ignore the problem. To compensate, I retreated to living mostly in my mind, focusing on my creative and intellectual life. But then, when you aren't in your body, when you aren't feral in some way, how can you create something real, something that has a heartbeat?

'During that marriage, despite writing all the time, I felt blocked and had trouble producing good writing. My writer's block only started lifting towards the end of the relationship, when I finally took a lover and came alive again. I don't think people who haven't found themselves in that type of situation would realise just how much not having sex affects other areas of your existence too.'

○ ○ ○

Mismatched libidos are only one reason for sexual attrition. What happens when both – or more – parties dearly want to have sex with each other and have access to a private-enough place to engage, but can't? That was the question facing Australian author Josephine Taylor and her now-husband John when, due to health issues, sex as they had previously known it became impossible.

Aged 39, working as a recently qualified psychotherapist with a growing clientele, and only a few months into her relationship with John, Josephine had her first run in with what would eventually be diagnosed as vulvodynia, a chronic and debilitating pain in the area around the opening of the vagina.

The condition features prominently in Josephine's 2021 novel *Eye of a Rook*, in which the stories of two women – one in the 21st century and one in the mid-19th century – intersect and inform each other. Despite the gulf of time and supposed progress separating the two women, they both have to contend with bafflement and misdiagnoses from (mostly male) doctors. The novel's descriptions of bodily pain are intensely visceral:

> It hurts like toothache that pierces the bones of your face and shoots through your thoughts, scattering them like frightened birds [...] It hurts like an earache that squats in your skull and scrawls graffiti on its walls, trashing the house that was once your home.[60]

I've not met Josephine in the flesh but recorded an episode of the popular *Words and Nerds* podcast with her in which we discussed representations of pain, desire and bodies in our respective novels. I was sad for the discussion to end and have felt that way every time we've corresponded since. When we speak for this book, Josephine is a few days into a residency at the Katharine Susannah Prichard Writers' Centre in Western Australia, while I'm – you guessed it – in my front room in Melbourne on Zoom.

Here's how Josephine describes the pain of vulvodynia now:

'In the early days, I thought I was the only person in the world who had this. Nobody had any idea of the pain. I mean, I've had kidney stones and I've had babies, and they're both pretty intense. But with this, even just the gentle movement of breathing, like when you breathe in and your belly moves down a tiny bit … it was so intense. I'd just have to lie down and stay very, very still for a long time.

'After a few months, when I realised it wasn't going away, I had to ring all my clients and tell them I couldn't see them anymore. I had to give up everything. I couldn't sit in a chair. It completely changed me as a mother and affected my relationship with my sons. I lost friends who couldn't go the distance with it.'

Though she and John were in the early stages of their adult relationship at the time, they had a past to draw on, having enjoyed 'very, very passionate encounters' with each other as teenagers.

'We had three nights together, separated by years,' Josephine remembers. 'The first was when we were 15 or 16 and camping at the same place in the bush. We were introduced by a friend and started kissing.

'There was another night a year or so later, when we were alone in a pool together at night and just had the most erotic time. And then there was a third time, where he wanted my phone number afterwards but never rang me. But I was just really, really in love with him.'

Like all good romantic comedies, they bumped into each other in unlikely places several times over the ensuing years but were both in other committed relationships, until eventually, on discovering she was single, John phoned Josephine, told her he was single too, and the pair threw more wood onto a fire that had been smouldering for a couple of decades.

'There's something that happens in your body at that young age when a sexual connection of that sort happens,' she says. 'It did something to our cells, something profound that lay the bedrock for our relationship later.'

The first big test came quickly. 'Initially, the pain was so bad that literally anything would make it worse,' she says. 'When we were still living separately, and John came round to visit, I'd get aroused and then be like, "Owwwww". That was really unpleasant. I thought "OK, well, I can't have intercourse but maybe I'm OK with giving myself pleasure", so I tried that but it was just excruciating the next day – there's usually a delay in the pain.'

It had a big effect on her self-perception, she says. 'A lot has changed in the last 20 years, but the idea back then was that the end goal of a heterosexual relationship was intercourse – that's what you're both heading towards, that's what you're supposed to want. That and other things, like simultaneous orgasms – all those ideals we're indoctrinated with. You feel you can't please your partner in the ways you've been taught you should. There's not only your own loss of pleasure but also the loss of what you want to be for your partner.'

During her first year with vulvodynia, she raised the prospect of the relationship ending. 'It was just too hard,' she says. 'I felt I couldn't carry him on top of carrying myself. But when I told him, he sort of said: "So I don't get any say in this?" He wouldn't let it go.' The result of which wasn't wholly unpleasant.

'I think when you have issues that affect your sexuality you have to work out the individual ways of giving each other pleasure,' she says. 'We're in a better place sexually now than we were 22 years ago because we've had to be honest and open with each other. We've had to connect in quite a deep way that takes account of the other person in all of their complexity.'

Josephine has written not just a novel but a PhD on women's experiences of vulvodynia, so knows exactly how prevalent it is (more than 8 per cent of women are thought to be affected by the condition at any one time). Yet she's still surprised how much the topic has resonated with people at her book events, during which women will often come up and tell her about their own stories of living with this type of pain. 'I respect other people's silence on this issue, I really do,' she says. 'But those kinds of responses have validated for me that it's really important to speak out and say, "fuck you, shame". Why is this something to be ashamed of? It's ridiculous.'

That there would be shame there in the first place goes much further than internalised ableism. In the 1866 section of *Eye of a Rook*, Josephine's character Emily Rochdale's vulvodynia is dismissed and misdiagnosed by her doctor variously as idiocy, epilepsy, a result of 'unnatural practices' (i.e. masturbation) and that most misogynistically judgy of all judgy Victorian diagnoses: hysteria. From the ancient Greek word for uterus, it was used as catch-all term for any and all female ailments and behaviours that made men feel uncomfortable.

'The shame most potently comes from it being about the genitals,' Josephine says. 'It's unseemly to talk about your genitals, for women particularly. There are times you can talk about sex, but it's got to be fantastic sex or vigorous sex. There are situations where you can be really out-there about all that stuff these days. But there's still a gold standard you have to meet.

'It used to really give me the shits, even before I had vulvodynia, the way sex and sexual pleasure for a female was portrayed in movies and so on. I've always had a bee in my bonnet about that. Whatever our gender or biology, we all seek pleasure in different ways, whether it's no sex or different kinds of sex – not this idea of a guy jumping on top of a woman who has an orgasm as soon as he puts his penis in.

'It's not only that it's inaccurate – it's that it then affects how people see themselves for generations. It affects how they think they should give and receive pleasure. That's always made me really cross.'

9
Role models

Rewatching 1980s and 90s American films with my kids has been a fraught experience in ways I'd not anticipated. Even those I'd remembered as impossibly wholesome – such as the 1988 family comedy *Big* – contain a level of male gaze and female objectification that now feels incredibly uncomfortable. Yes, it's an inherently creepy plot – a 12-year-old boy in a man's body has sex with a grown woman – but I'd forgotten that part and, as a kid, I wasn't knowingly aware of the lascivious boob shots. Likewise, I was seemingly oblivious to all those moments in other films when the male leads force themselves on women who, after a perfunctory struggle, capitulate and want to be kissed. But it all goes in.

Something I've noticed with my kids, especially when they were younger, is that whatever they're watching they do so wide-eyed, the sound and vision drenching their spongy brains – a phenomenon described by developmental psychologist Alison Gopnik as 'lantern consciousness'. The idea is that everything children can see, in both their direct and peripheral vision, is illuminated more brightly than it is for adults to allow for maximum absorption.[61]

When they were five and six watching – at my behest – the corny 1980 action film *Flash Gordon*, they didn't say 'Holy crap, Daddy, these special effects are so bad,' nor did they seem to have the sense that Flash would obviously win the day because that's how every hero's journey ends. Judging by their faces, this was a real story playing out in real time with all the surprise and sense of jeopardy filmmakers want us to feel, and none of the jadedness that comes with repeat exposure.

In that same era, I remember my youngest son being confused and then astounded when I explained that some animated films were made from drawings – he didn't think of them as anything other than 'real' because they were, even in the case of talking lions and elephants, realistic.

How much more realistic must it have been for them seeing Princess Aura in *Flash Gordon*, showing Flash in a cramped cockpit how to 'work the controls', whispering lines like 'gently darling, it's extremely sensitive, like me'?[62] Or for me at a similar age watching Princess Leia in chains and a skimpy bikini, grimacing as her collar was repeatedly yanked by Jabba the Hutt.

We grow up, of course, and might laughingly recall how a near-naked Carrie Fisher played a part in our sexual awakening – but what messages were being communicated by those chains, the subservience, the fact the only female Star Wars lead was sexualised and degraded in ways Luke Skywalker and Han Solo never were?

Representation has come a long way and the male gaze (with countless exceptions) is no longer the automatically unchallenged norm. Some of us, maybe most of us, laughed when the hapless Lloyd asked Mary in the 1994 film *Dumb and Dumber* what his chances were of winning her affection:

Mary: Not good.

Lloyd: Do you mean not good like one out of a hundred?

Mary: I'd say more like one out of a million.

Lloyd, after a long pause: So, you're telling me there's a chance?[63]

Lloyd persists, of course, and wins Mary's affection despite being a ghoulish stalker because that's the kind of disbelief we're urged to suspend time and again. Fewer of us laughed when the real-life British man Luke Howard made global headlines in 2017 for buying a piano and playing it non-stop on College Green in Bristol, UK, in a bid to win back his former girlfriend (of four months) who had recently (can't think why) dumped him. A whack job, right? But was it substantially any different to trench coat-wearing Lloyd Dobler in 1989's *Say Anything* obnoxiously (sorry, charmingly) holding a boombox over his head outside the bedroom window of Diane Court to win her affection?

Stories have always been a two-way street, informed by and informing the way we see ourselves and the world around us. Which is all the more reason to champion diversity and sensitivity in the stories we tell and the people telling and commissioning them.

It's harder than it was – but still not impossible – to imagine an ensemble comedy like 2003's *Love Actually* being made in the 2020s, presenting multiple romances between almost exclusively heterosexual, monogamous people while blissfully ignoring its central (and demonstrably true) argument that love is, actually, all around. Yes, ageing rock star Billy Mack and his manager Joe decide to spend Christmas night together getting drunk and watching porn but it's hardly *Call Me by Your Name*.

Of course, take away the assumption that heterosexual monogamy resuting in marriage is the be-all and end-all of life and most rom-coms would grind to a halt. The idea that 2001's *Bridget Jones's Diary* could end with Bridget not having to choose between Daniel and Mark but pursuing an ongoing relationship with both *is* raised momentarily, but only to set up a punchine about ice-cream:

> **Bridget:** I'm enjoying a relationship with two men simultaneously. The first called Ben, the other Jerry.[64]

Whether or not they end well or badly (it's badly), such love triangles are a staple of the stories we like to tell ourselves. *A Tale of Two Cities, Gone with the Wind, The Great Gatsby, The Hunger Games, Vicky Cristina Barcelona, Titanic* ... Our protagonist is desired by or desirous of more than one person and a choice must be made.

Where consensual nonmonogamy creeps up in modern stories, it still tends to be a morality tale, allowing us to indulge in a bit of transgressive titillation before our protagonists come to their senses.

The 2018 BBC drama *Wanderlust* explored the opening up of Joy and Steven's marriage only to reveal that Joy's promiscuity was symptomatic of trauma and that monogamy was always – in case anyone doubted – the correct course of action. Just as well for Joy, really, as she probably wouldn't have survived otherwise.

'In *Anna Karenina*, Anna throws herself in front of a train,' Rochelle Siemienowicz says. 'Lady Chatterley ends up pregnant and unhappy.

'With the novel I'm writing currently, I'm trying to create a story that challenges those narratives and seems a bit truer to what I've experienced in my life as a poly person. What if Anna Karenina was able to still have a happy family with her husband as well as the excitement of a lover? What if Madame Bovary didn't poison herself and die horribly? There are only a couple of stories out there of a woman living happily with two men as far as I know but they're real esoterica. I want to tell that story and be honest about the hard work that's involved, the reality and not the fairy tale.

'All kinds of love and family relationships are possible and we need to see them represented in culture.'

As I mentioned earlier in this book, some poly people seemed slightly annoyed with me because the characters in my novel *Poly* were bad role models for polyamory. As I wrote at the time for *Herald Scotland*:

Claiming to understand polyamory through fictional descriptions of the sort seen in the Netflix series *You Me Her* would be like basing your entire philosophy of friendship on the 1990s sitcom *Friends*.[65]

Reflecting now, I think it's a scarcity issue. In that same article, I wrote that mine was 'the first realist polyamory novel to be published in Australia, and one of a relative handful in the world'. Because of that, it maybe carried, and inevitably failed to meet, certain expectations. As far as I know, bestselling American author Sue Miller's 2020 novel *Monogamy*, about a married couple of 30 years, wasn't criticised for failing to comprehensively portray monogamy. And why would it be? There are many thousands of other monogamy stories out there.

○ ○ ○

Roz Bellamy is talking about an essay the late Melbourne-based writer Kat Muscat wrote for the literary journal *Kill Your Darlings* in 2014 called 'Ain't Love Grand': The Erasure of Bisexuality in Buffy the Vampire Slayer'. The essay interrogates the coming out as lesbian of the character Willow Rosenberg in the '90s show – with her iconic line 'Hello, gay now' – and the simultaneous turning away from her previous, hetero-seeming self. As Muscat wrote:

> Willow is relegated to the binary of totally straight/totally gay. The implicit message is that Willow's homosexuality can only be legitimate so long as it is completely free of lusty emotions for the opposite sex. This particular oversimplification of non-heterosexual identity persists in the media even as we are granted more gay characters.[66]

'That really impacted me,' Roz says. '*Buffy* had been one of the cultural markers that really helped with my sexual awakening. I remember that piece being important to me, and I've gone on to write about Willow in my memoir as well.'

While Roz has found themselves being 'kind of sick of the representation conversation', they know it's still valuable, especially if it comes with an awareness of intersectionality – the idea that we're not just one thing but a Venn diagram with overlapping circles that inform each other, amplifying or lessening the barriers we face and/or privileges we enjoy.

'I now see the layers to it as opposed to early on when I was very much like "representation is good and no representation is bad",' they say. 'There's so much to think about beyond sexual identity – factors like class and race and disability.

'In terms of gender-diverse representation, there are people that come to mind for me in TV, movies and books, but none where I'm like, "Wow, if I'd had that person growing up all this would have been so easy for me". I don't think I have that at all.'

Which is not to say those representations don't help (or hinder) in more tangential ways. 'In the TV show *Billions*, there's a non-binary character, and I know for my parents that was instrumental because the character uses they–them pronouns. The other characters just effortlessly use those pronouns when they're referring to that character, whereas in real life people get it wrong all the time or stumble over it. It's that sort of thing where a show leads to conversations that a person may or may not be ready to have with family.

'But because there are such limited depictions, your family or significant people in your life might also be watching those shows and making certain assumptions about you too, and that's complicated. As with any marginalised identity, you can find yourself watching with a little bit of discomfort, wondering what mainstream viewers are going to take away from them.'

Even the most evolved fictional characters are going to look like cardboard cut-outs next to people in real life, who don't – on the whole – come with mapped-out backstories and narrative arcs, and who shift and resettle as frequently as they need to.

'Sometimes "gender-diverse" fits me more, sometimes "agender",' Roz says. 'But for me it mostly comes down to an apathy to there being any sort of differentiation between male and female. Sometimes notions of femininity and masculinity are appealing to me but other times I feel a strong resistance to them or even a sense of revulsion.'

Getting that right in terms of the stories we tell is likely to be as complicated and contentious as discussions about gender are in living rooms and online, but that's precisely *why* such stories are important.

'When it comes to gender, some cisgender people seem to feel wronged or wounded by people who question the binary,' they say. 'It's as if we're shaking up everything people believe in – it elicits the same sort of emotions patriotic Australians feel towards those of us who are against Australia Day and flying the flag.

'There's still a sense that, if you don't follow your genitals, your biological construct, there's something wrong with your brain.'

Archer, the magazine Roz edits – billed as the 'world's most inclusive magazine about sexuality, gender and identity' – is of course its own juggernaut of representation.

'One of the things I've always found interesting at *Archer* is looking at the web analytics and seeing what things people look at most. Pieces about bisexuality always do well, as do pieces about polyamory.

'Sometimes we'll get questions from readers like, "Why don't you have more articles from people in the adult diaper-wearing community?" and we're like, "We would publish those articles, but we're just not finding people who want to write them, and particularly who want to put their name on them".

'But that's changing. Even if I'm not optimistic about broader society, I feel optimistic about the writing world, where there's so much celebration of diversity.

'People are now writing about things that would previously have been seen as extremely taboo or would make them feel there was something quite wrong with them because they'd been psychopathologised. Knowing those people are in a place where they can either put their name on articles or are very close to it is very exciting in terms of agency and subjectivity.'

○ ○ ○

Dr Whitney Monaghan works in Communications and Media Studies at Monash University and is the co-author of the 2019 book *Queer Theory Now: From Foundations to Futures.*

For the last few years, she's been researching the representation of sexuality on Australian TV, mainly from the 1970s to the turn of the millennium, looking specifically at characters identified within the shows as gay, lesbian or bisexual – the findings of which might seem counterintuitive.

'Australian television in the 1970s was world-leading with its representation of gay and bisexual characters,' she says. *Number 96* and *The Box* were two incredibly popular and controversial series in that era, known for their sensationalised and sexy storylines. When *Number 96* was first broadcast, the advertisements read "Tonight at 8.30. Television loses its virginity".

'Between them, those two shows introduced the first gay character in a soap opera, the first kiss between women on primetime television, and likely also the first trans character played by a trans actor, Carlotta.'

Though those characters and storylines were consistent with the sensationalist aspirations of the shows, they were popular for other, more heartening reasons too. 'My research involved reading a lot of television magazines and TV guides and I saw several letters to the editor where readers were defending the inclusion of storylines about same-sex relationships,' Whitney says.

There were also numerous crime dramas featuring gay, lesbian or bisexual characters, although calling them positive representations would be yogi-level stretch. 'In the mid 1970s, the popular series *Homicide* had an episode about a lesbian couple that had a secret torture chamber in their basement and another about a gay couple that were antique furniture thieves.'

1980s and '90s shows – among them *Prisoner, A Country Practice, Pacific Drive* – included some one-off and ongoing gay and lesbian characters, Whitney says, but there was less emphasis – and consequently less press about – those. 'In the 1990s, it was actually quite difficult to find the characters and stories without having to watch hundreds of hours of television,' she says. 'But overall, Australian television in that period shifted its representation of lesbian, gay and bisexual characters from villains and victims to "respectable" and accepted members of society, with more stories where sexuality wasn't really the issue.'

Whitney points to 2016's *Seeing Ourselves*, Screen Australia's landmark report on diversity on screen, which found that LGBTQIA+ characters made up about 5 per cent of all TV characters at the time.[67]

'The contemporary situation is a bit more promising,' she says. 'But Australian TV is still quite conservative when it comes to representing queer characters and stories. Some of our great series in recent years have been *Wentworth, Please Like Me* and *The Newsreader*, and when talking about trans stories it's hard to go past ABC's *First Day*. But most of the queer-themed content is being produced for the ABC, SBS, and streamers such as Foxtel. Commercial broadcast is lagging by quite a lot.'

A notable exception being the 2021 edition of Network 10's reality dating show *The Bachelorette*, starring Brooke Blurton. 'That season featured the show's first Indigenous and "bisexual" person, though I believe she identifies as pansexual. This was a ground-breaking series, featuring both male and female suitors in what I believe was a great representation of bisexuality.

'I watched it as it was broadcast and loved it. Afterwards, I caught an episode of *Gogglebox*, the reality program about watching TV. I can't remember who said it, but I distinctly remember one of the cast members commenting that "Men are going to love this". There was a suggestion that the sight of women kissing would be the main selling point of the series, so clearly that attitude is still circulating. I'm not sure we've fully escaped the thrall of the male gaze.'

One solution, or part of the solution, might be a Richard Curtis-style festive film in which the opening monologue goes something like this:

> Lots of people love someone. Films and books tend to present it in a hackneyed way but just look around – two men cuddling, a thruple playing frisbee, a bisexual cousin at a barbecue, boyfriends, girlfriends, husbands, wives, asexual aunts and uncles, queer and straight friends. If you want to, I'm almost certain you'll see there are many kinds of love, actually.

'I'm probably being a bit cynical, but I do think the majority of main-stream films continue to uphold quite traditional conservative values when it comes to love, sex and relationships,' Whitney says. 'We're probably still a little way off from the Christmas romcom featuring an intricate web of poly relationships – though I would absolutely go to see that in an instant.'

○ ○ ○

Pop music has long been progressive with its signifiers, from the glam rock of T-Rex to the androgyny of Annie Lennox, from the S&M stylings of Rihanna to the powder-pink cowboy aesthetic of Lil Nas X, from Janelle Monáe to Harry Styles. For me, it's always been the most encouraging art form, a world in which fluidity and ambiguity are – literally – amped up, a glittery reminder that gender is performative.

For the last few years I've worn eye make-up semi-regularly. Initially it was applied by my partner, Kate, while I blinked and tried not to hyperventilate at the thought of her accidentally stabbing my eyeball with her sharpened eye pencil, but increasingly I apply it myself. I have my favourite shades – brown, green and purple pencils work best with my eye colour. I know my way around the Gwen Stefani eyeshadow range and can just about apply mascara without it clumping on my lashes. Honestly, when I see the results, I can't believe more men, all men, don't wear make-up. Talk about missing a trick. My aesthetic is informed by Bowie (always), Martin Gore from Depeche Mode (often), Adam Ant (hells yeah) and Brett Anderson from Suede. I remember where I was when I first saw each of those performers on TV, the feeling of goosebumps and the deep longing to look as slinky and sexy as them.

To go with the make-up, Kate enjoys (very much, she says) dressing me in clothes from the women's section in shops, some of which she buys for me specifically, some of which are hers. This is for mostly for parties, not for work, but hey, you never know!

At those parties, the most noticeable thing for me, apart from women friends complimenting Kate's handiwork, is a confusion among some of the menfolk. One occasion stands out in particular. I was in a gold chainmail dress, heels, feathery fake lashes and a shoulder-length blonde wig.

'Who are you tonight?' asked a man I'd known for years.

'Um, just me,' I said.

An hour or so later, the same man said: 'Seriously though, who are you? Do you have a name?'

'It's me – Paul,' I whispered, pulling my synthetic fringe to one side so he could get a better look.

'But … But all this,' he said, pointing at the dress and my excellent (if I say so myself) thighs hewn from thousands of hours of pre-lockdown-era cycling. 'What's your character?'

'Pretty much dour Scotsman,' I said. 'Same as usual, really.'

I'd been, it seemed, transformed beyond recognition, my face funda-mentally the same, limbs and torso unaltered, voice unchanged, but rendered strange and unknowable by a gold dress, wig and some lashes. I've always seen pop music and the androgeny of my idols as a quick way to shake up assumptions about who we are and who we can be so, in some ways, I was delighted to confound this man.

It was a small part, of course, in a much broader shake-up.

'Vanilla sex is not as stable and as enshrined as it used to be,' Jinghua Qian says. 'From reading and from talking to straight co-workers and others, I've got the sense that the way heterosexual people have sex has become queerer and more diverse.

'You can definitely see that in popular culture, in music videos. A lot of kink culture has become really mainstream as an aesthetic and practice. If you listen to pop songs now, half of them are really fuck-ing kinky. Some of that is at a superficial aesthetic level – you know, whips and chains look cool so let's all put them in our music videos – but I think there's something deeper going on there too.

'Obviously, as a queer person, I'm more aware of what queers are doing, but I can hardly think of any young celebrities who present as straight – like, that now seems deeply uncool. Maybe there are some straight ones, but that almost feels like it would be a funny perfor-mance, that it would be like drag.

'I could definitely imagine a young teenager now coming out as straight, especially to queer parents but also to straight parents. There's still a norm but vanilla is no longer the thing to necessarily aspire to.'

○ ○ ○

Somehow, it's never occurred to me that Shakespeare and his characters would be LGBTQIA+ role models, even though he wrote homoerotic sonnets and plays drenched with gender fluidity – not least *Twelfth Night*. By way of brief synopsis:

Parted from her twin brother, Sebastian, Viola dresses up as a boy and finds work with Duke Orsino, with whom she falls in love. Alas, he's in love with Countess Olivia and urges Viola to put in a good word for him. But when Viola does that, the countess falls in love with her, thinking her a man. Sebastian shows up and eventually marries Countess Olivia, while Viola – now a woman again – marries Duke Orsino.

'My whole 13 years of primary and secondary education were in the Catholic system,' Julie Peters says. 'Gender non-conformity was really looked down upon. Boys who might have been gay, or even slightly feminine, were ostracised.

'This is still 40 years before the internet, and in the one or two films I'd seen where a male dressed as a woman, they were something to be laughed at, or bashed. Sadly, that was the case right up until about 1992, which is already after I transitioned – if there was a trans person in a film, they were either murdered, were themselves the murderer, or they suicided.

'I didn't find any positive role models at a young age. But the Catholic education system, a little inadvertently I think now, worshipped Shakespeare, like almost everybody did in the '50s and '60s. And so, we read *Twelfth Night*. The first thing we were told was that, in Shakespeare's day, it was considered poor taste for a woman to go on stage, so boys always played the female roles. I was sitting there thinking, "Oh, wow, that would be amazing. I'd love to be a Shakespearean actor".

'In *Twelfth Night*, you have this crazy situation where a boy plays a girl who then disguises herself as a boy. And then a woman played by a boy falls for this boy who's really a girl played by a boy.

'I found it really interesting that the teachers never commented on any of this, only the stuff about women not being allowed to act.

'Because it was a working-class Catholic school, our teachers didn't really expect us to understand it. They'd get us to read bits of the play in class, and then explained things as we went along. I just loved it.'

○ ○ ○

Omar Sakr says he had few, if any, workable examples to follow growing up. I put to him that, as a poet and novelist writing about queerness from an Arab–Australian perspective, he might at least be providing that for other people now. But even as I ask it, I have Holden Sheppard's words still ringing in my ears about the burden of being co-opted as a role model. Does Omar feel that too?

'I feel a responsibility only to truth,' he says. 'If I'm honest about who I am, about my faults and fears, loves and losses, then I'm confident I can be of good service to my communities.

'I assumed the pose early on of hoping that my public queerness would be helpful to others because there were no high-profile queer Arab–Australian Muslims to look to, but truthfully, at the time, I was operating in a daze of suicidal ideation and depression. I assumed I wasn't going to live long anyway so I was happy to risk it all.

'I was also unable to have the conversation with my family and hoped that by being honest online I would eventually be discovered. As most of my relatives are un- or under-educated, not online, and certainly not readers, this didn't actually pan out even as my profile grew.

'It's only more recently, as my financial position stabilised and I was able to get help, to get my mental health on track, that I can say I'm truly living the ethos I first described. Consciously and positively, I am here for my peoples.'

In many ways, Omar says, he only feels like he's been alive in the last nine years, much of which he attributes to finding his purpose in poetry, as taught by Judith Beveridge at the University of Sydney. That and a sense of communion with a long list of writers, including Ali Cobby Eckermann, David Malouf, Naomi Shihab Nye, Najwan Darwish and Christos Tsiolkas, who have provided comfort and inspiration in recent years – positive (or simply authentic) role models, in other words.

'I could go on and on,' he says. 'I'm so blessed to have met, worked with, or simply to have read the words of these legends and I still look to them today.'

10
Help, I'm alive

Am I queer? I've been thinking about this for some time and the short answer is: I don't think so.

Have I experienced the types of othering, oppression and fear of physical and emotional harm as someone who is out – or has been outed – as queer? Or, indeed, the particular camaraderie, laughter and positive shared life experiences? As a straight (with potential caveats) white able-bodied cis man, it's hard not to answer with a capitalised NO WAY. By those measures I am, in fact, the opposite of queer, the very thing it defines itself in contrast to.

Which hasn't stopped me asking the internet questions like 'Is polyamory queer?' on occasion. In forums and blogs there are as many versions of the answer 'GET STUFFED, YOU'RE DREAMING' as there are of 'Well, actually, you might be ...'

When I googled it recently, the first result was a Medium article by a writer called Kim Barrett with the headline: 'Does Polyamory Fall Under the LGBT+ Umbrella?' Barrett, who identifies as both poly and LGBT+, writes that:

> Polyamory should stand shoulder to shoulder with the LGBT+ community, rather than within it, and we should both continue to challenge society to rethink what a relationship looks like.[68]

This seems about right to me, but I want to know what others think, not least Dr Jessica Kean, who – like Barrett – has experienced life in both LGBTQIA+ and poly contexts.

'Some experiences of being poly can feel equivalent to being queer,' she says. 'I remember going ice-skating with both of my partners, in one of those places with disco music. There was a moment when the DJ said, "This song's just for the lovers", meaning everyone else should sit down while the couples skated around.

'The three of us ended up on the sidelines feeling uncomfortable. We didn't quite feel we could stand up and hold hands and all skate around together, so we self-excluded and then sat there fuming. That's what a lot of queer folk who weren't confident they were in a safe environment would also feel in that moment – they'd go from happily skating to having to decide whether or not to tell everyone in the room about the nature of their relationship.'

In her PhD research, Jessica spoke to a range of folk, from LGBTQIA+ polyamorous people who identified as queer, to heterosexual poly people who also identified as queer, to other hetero people who saw polyamory as a take-it-or-leave-it lifestyle choice. As per the ongoing debate online, there was no clear consensus. I know Jessica's not *that* kind of doctor, but I wonder how she might diagnose me.

'I guess my feeling is you don't need to be queer,' she says. 'I'm not saying you are or not, but I don't think you have to be queer to be having a significant experience of falling outside of really important social norms that people care a lot about. People who are openly nonmonogamous have meaningful things in common with the experiences of queer folk without it being totally the same thing, in my opinion.

'When you're in a nonmonogamous relationship, especially as publicly as you've been because of your book, then you're dealing with people's intrusive ideas and assumptions about your relationship.

Potentially you're also dealing with a lot of stigma and shaming about your relationship choices.'

○ ○ ○

I'm hoping Australian author, relationship expert and sex counsellor Jane Roder can offer some further clarity – her website promises 'breakthrough conversations to take your relationships and your sex life to another level'.

We're talking on Zoom about the multiple ways we sabotage ourselves and others with whom we're in a relationship.

'There are many factors,' Jane says. 'But the stories we take on about ourselves are what ultimately create us.

'Aristotle's saying 'Give me a child until he is seven and I will show you the man' has a lot of truth to it. Stories about love and relationships are imprinted on us during childhood, with the parents' or guardians' relationship as the model of love we see and take on. As an adult, you're still going to be living into that, depending on how you've created your stories.'

Much of the work Jane does with clients involves resurfacing and unpicking those narratives, with an emphasis on the individual taking responsibility for their unwanted patterns of behaviour. Mostly, in her work on sexuality, she sees heterosexual people, with only a handful of LGBTQIA+ clients.

She specialises in 'couples' therapy, which is making me a little nervous to ask about people in thruples, quads and quintets.

'Society pushes this idea that the more sex we have, the happier we'll be,' Jane says. 'There's the myth that the more orgasms you have, the happier you'll be. The myth that men have to have a six-pack and a hard dick, and it's got to be a big dick to please a woman. The myth that women have to look gorgeous and sexually please a man to be loved. There's all this stuff circulating. Everybody seems to be having good sex except us – that's another myth. That it's OK to be with lots of different partners ...'

As Jane circles ever closer to the idea of multi-person set-ups, I want to ask about monogamy – whether (as per the 2002 book *The Myth of Monogamy*) it's just another inherited lie. I want to ask, as per *Sex at Dawn*, about agrarian reform and the process by which monogamy became enmeshed with understandings about people – i.e. women – as chattel. About the archaic word 'rapine', meaning the violent seizure of someone's property, and how we still use a derivative of that in law and society for a sexual crime committed against (primarily) women and girls.

I think my mind wants to change the subject because Jane seems to be suggesting that it's not OK to be with lots of different partners, and my brain is equating that with a veiled criticism of me and the fact that, as Jane and I are chatting, my wife and partner are in the next room playing UNO with the kids. I can hear them all laughing – they seem fine. But are they? Am I harming anyone, maybe everyone, with my reckless behaviour? Jane has said nothing of the sort. So why am I feeling so bloody defensive?

Maybe it's a product of something she outlined earlier, that 'what we get upset by 90 per cent of the time comes from our pasts'.

So what, from my past, is pushing me into thinking – or amplifying my existing thoughts – that I'm doing something wrong? Unlike a great many of my friends growing up, my parents didn't separate or divorce, although, in truth, they probably should have. My mum was clearly unhappy in the last few years of her relationship and life. She'd get excited talking to me and my sister about aspirations and goals she had that were eminently achievable – until the focus shifted back to the fact those ambitions would entail leaving my dad. The maxim she repeated was the one her father (who was married for close to 70 years) had passed on to her: 'It's not real happiness if it makes someone else unhappy.'

He didn't mean cheering for your sporting team at the expense of their opponents. He meant that staying married and accepting your lot was what you did, regardless of how uninspiring or outright awful the union was – a philosophy of quiet despair.

As a grown adult, I have to say the idea of choosing to remain unhappy to avoid making your partner unhappy ranks right up there with the craziest advice I've ever heard. It's self-defeating and doesn't even work.

My mum's secondary, connected mantra was that my dad wouldn't be able to cope without her. Then she died, giving him no option but to manage without her, without pursuing the very things that would have made her life seem worth living. I'd like to think, then, that the 'sacrifice your happiness and protect your marriage at all costs' story doesn't inform my own beliefs about relationships, but I think it probably does. It doesn't even matter that I see it as stupid.

When I was a boy, to keep me safe, my mum told me that train tracks were electrified and that if you stood on one when a train was less than a mile away, you'd be fried to a crisp. She never got round to telling me it was a white lie – I came to that realisation myself, eventually. But even now, decades later, I wince and withdraw my foot quickly any time I accidently step on a train or tram track.

'I haven't actually worked with anyone in a polyamorous relationship,' Jane says. 'But I have had cases where one half of a couple wants to explore polyamory and their partner is not prepared to do that. Sometimes that leads to them splitting up. My experience is that most people aren't capable of polyamory on an emotional level. On a biological level, we're not monogamous creatures. I mean, that's true on an animal level, but we're not animals, right?'

The 1967 book *The Naked Ape: A Zoologist's Study of the Human Animal* bounds into my mind unannounced, beating its chest and making those oo-oo primate noises. I interviewed its author, the English zoologist Desmond Morris in the mid-noughties at his home in Oxfordshire.

What I remember most clearly from the interview is Morris telling me about his longstanding friendship with the actor Marlon Brando, who contacted him out of the blue on the phone in the middle of the night once to ask if they could discuss the nature of violence. I imagine Morris's response might have been something like this passage from his book:

> Much of what we do as adults is based on ... imitative absorption during our childhood years. Frequently we imagine that we are behaving in a particular way because such behaviour accords with some abstract, lofty code of moral principles, when in reality all we are doing is obeying a deeply ingrained and long 'forgotten' set of purely imitative impressions (along with our carefully concealed instinctive urges) that makes it so hard for societies to change their customs and their "beliefs".[69]

'On a social, emotional and spiritual level, monogamy serves us well,' Jane says. 'It's the best thing we've got. Marriage is what best serves the children – it's better for people's health and finances.

'People think there's more chance of a monogamous relationship having infidelity or breaking down but what I see is that it's harder to maintain multiple partners. Most people haven't got the capacity. Like me personally – I couldn't do it. We're not saying that's wrong or right, just that it's very difficult for most people to do.'

○○○

Chris Cheers is a psychologist and author of the 2023 book *The New Rulebook*. I first came across him and his work on social media, where he has a large and engaged following for good reason: he helps people with their mental health.

Identifying openly as queer and poly differentiates him from most people in his profession.

'I've worked pretty extensively over the last ten years with LGBTIQ populations, especially trans and gender-diverse populations,' he says. 'Supporting people through Covid in recent years, and having this real sense that psychologists are incredibly overworked and needed, I've become really interested in making mental health and wellbeing ideas more accessible. Through social media, I saw I could reach more than just the number of people I could see in my private practice, and that's also where I started to discover the power of writing.'

While *The New Rulebook* was originally going to be exclusively focused on mental health and wellbeing advice and strategies for LGBTQIA+ people, that soon changed. 'I became quite interested in the idea that there are more similarities between people who are queer and people who aren't than differences,' he says. 'It's not like the strategies are immensely different in a queer relationship versus a straight one, or for one queer person versus another. A lot of the evidence-based strategies in psychology are basically the same – they just change a bit depending on the individual.

'Because the way we work and love and look at mental health has changed over the last few years, I thought we needed a new rulebook.'

I'm heartened by all of this – how could anyone not be? – but I also want to know what Chris thinks was wrong with the previous rule-books. 'Lots of the ideas we've inherited about mental health and wellbeing are perhaps not as helpful as we think they are,' he says. 'They're quite grounded in white Western philosophy and a heter-onormative idea of mental health and wellbeing. If you're outside of that, there's often a view that either you're doing something wrong that needs to be fixed or you need a specialist service.

'That has to be challenged. It's unhelpful for clients to get the message that what they're doing is wrong just because it's misunderstood or not in the psychologist's experience.

'I started my career almost trying to be a robot, to be "like a psychologist" and not bring myself into the room. But as I've embraced my queerness and other parts of my identity, I've been able to bring that to the space in a way that's not counterproductive to the clients' work.

'I've heard from the people I work with time and again that they feel a sense of acceptance and connection because I'm being genuine. I've started realising I'm in a rare position as a psychologist who studied relationship therapy and works with queer populations, who is also queer and poly.'

As such, Chris is not only intellectually but physically connected to concepts such as minority stress, whereby people who belong to stigmatised minority groups face chronically high levels of stress. 'Being trans or queer, you're more likely to have mental health challenges,' he says. 'It's the outcome of being a minority surrounded by a family or workplace or society that sees you as lesser. That's something I deal with a lot with my clients.

'There's this sense that people are now more accepting of people who are LGBTIQA+, but it's one thing to accept, another to include that person in your family or life as much as you would anyone else. A lot of people are dealing with discrimination and judgement.

'If you've received the message from a young age that you're "less than" it can translate to a low sense of self-worth. It becomes difficult for people to have confidence and see themselves compassionately when they've internalised those things, and those feelings and patterns of behaviour can carry through into their relationships. I want to show acceptance in my work, but also to dismantle the self-judgement and internalised homophobia or transphobia that have been perpetuated throughout a person's life.'

Like many others, Chris uses 'queer' as an umbrella term for LGBTQIA+ people. 'For me, it's useful for anything you can define as being against the norm,' he says. 'The beauty of that is we get to create our own lives that work for us and can act against expectations of who we should be. But it also takes a huge amount of work when you have to create your own language or make your way through life without much in the way of models or help around you.'

As the language evolves, are relationships evolving too? 'There are new terms and labels being used all the time to describe different genders and sexualities,' he says. 'Within the LGBTQ+ population, where most of my clients come from, I'm seeing an increase in consensual nonmonogamy, and that follows the data. The last time I looked, about 50 per cent of queer relationships now have some sort of communicated understanding of sex outside the relationship, and that's growing. But I think what's on the increase is not so much the act of doing it but having the language to talk about it.

'For many years, people have been having sex outside their relationships, and often we call that an affair or cheating. But people are moving away from that quite restrictive view and starting to explore those ideas. Ten years ago, in my part of queer Australia, nonmonogamy wasn't really talked about in the same way, but I think there's an increasing acceptance.'

Being polyamorous has informed Chris's views and depth of understanding in ways reading about it probably never could. As if hearing the question I haven't asked yet, he responds to my grandad and mum's mantra about rejecting your own happiness if it comes at the cost of your partner's.

'Being poly has taught me that we often view other people's reactions and emotions to us as the indicator of whether what we're doing is right or wrong,' he says. 'When it comes to exploring poly, that can be really challenging because you will upset people for sure. Your friends will be like, "What are you doing?", as will your family. There's this understanding that if you're doing something that's hurting your partner or causing them to have negative emotions then you should stop doing it.'

So, what can you do if, like me, you're an inveterate people pleaser? I'm as likely to stop trying to find ways to prevent others from feeling uncomfortable as I am to stop biting my nails, which I've been doing since I've had teeth.

'You need to sit down with your partner and discuss the kind of relationship you want, and then acknowledge that uncomfortable, challenging emotions are often going to be a normal part of trying to get to that – they're not an indicator that something you're doing is wrong.'

As we're chatting, I can't stop thinking that Chris must be excellent with his clients. His calm and supportive presence feels both genuine and backed up by research. Which is why I feel bold enough to ask the question I've been struggling with, even though it spills out clumsily as several in quick succession. If you're heterosexual and polyamorous, are you queer? Is calling yourself queer in those circumstances a weird appropriation? Can a straight white cis man ever genuinely be marginalised for his sexuality or relationship choices in the Anglosphere?

'I can take parts of all those questions, I think,' Chris says. See – what a champ. 'Basically, as you've said, if you're white, straight and cisgendered, there's a path you're meant to be on and as long as you stay on it, more or less, you're going to have a power privilege, at least within Australian society. It's really helpful to notice that the more you step out of that path in terms of your identity, each difference will add more discrimination.

'As soon as you identify as a trans person, you're going to have to deal with discrimination. But you're going to deal with even more discrimination if you're a person of colour who is trans. The research shows that discrimination is not just additive – it multiplies depending on the intersections.

'As a white cis-gendered man in a poly relationship, there's an othering and a stigma, but that's going to be nothing compared to someone
who has all these different levels where they're othered because of
their identity.'

I think what I'm hearing is that I'm not queer, which tallies with what
I've suspected all along. I should go get my straighty-180 T-shirt, sit
in the garden, embrace my heteronormativity. But, no, it's not quite
that simple.

'While it's important to understand and honour each part of the
LGBTQIA+ rainbow, it's also useful to acknowledge what things might
be similar amongst queer people as a whole,' Chris says. 'One of which
is that we're working against the idea of hegemonic masculinity and
the idea that the white cis-gendered male is power. It's about stepping
outside of any of those norms that are given privilege.

'There are different views, but I think consensual nonmonogamy and
anything else under that umbrella is an example of queerness, just as
when I walk into a grocery store in a sequined dress I'm queering the
space. It's not just about sexuality – it's about doing something that
acts against the norm.'

11
The nuclear option

Hey there! Looking for a pre-approved relationship model? Something smart but not too flashy? You can't beat the nuclear family. Its popularity is such that you only need to think 'family' and, boop, it's right there in your mind.

Yes, the heteronormative ideal of 2.4 kids has diminished slightly, with 1.9 kids now the average for Australian couples with children, but the long-lauded notion of Mum, Dad and (almost) two biological kids is smudged like Vegemite into the nation's fabric.

The Merriam-Webster dictionary dates the first use of 'nuclear family' to 1924 – some 21 years before the detonation of the first nuclear bomb – but the structure, according to DNA testing of Stone Age burials, goes back at least four and a half thousand years. Should we perish in a nuclear winter, when future generations sift through the detritus of our doomed age they'll discover nuclear families were still alive and well in the 2020s: two adults and 1.9 kids, or the outlines of them imprinted on stone, huddling together until the end.

The nuclear was living cheek by jowl with the extended family in Europe long before the first pox-ridden ships arrived in Australia, rising to dominance alongside the first baby-steps of industrialisation. And in many ways, that continues. Political campaigns are built on the nuclear family. Tax cuts are aimed at it. Ads for cars, restaurants and holidays reinforce it. Stories for kids and adults regurgitate it. Society decorates it. Schools celebrate it.

And yet, it's a minority position. Data from the 2021 Census shows 43.7 per cent of Australian families comprise couples with children, a percentage eclipsed by the joint total of couples with no children (38.8 per cent) and lone parent families (15.9 per cent).[70] Polyamorous families with or without kids weren't counted, of course – and even if they were ... well, they just weren't.

In 2017, I stopped seeing the therapist I'd been visiting regularly after an outburst that embarrassed us both. We'd been meeting in a comfy office every Friday morning for eleven weeks, an appointment I'd started to rely on and look forward to even though I often left feeling raw and teary. It's amazing the things you get used to.

One morning, as I was talking about my kids and how they'd been happy at the beach the previous weekend with Kate, Jess and me, the therapist barked:

'It isn't fair on your kids.'

I stopped blabbering, unsure what to say or do next. My immediate internal reaction was something along the lines of: 'Shit, she's right, whatever the "it" refers to, *it's* unfair, *it* must be, that thing I'm doing, *it's* wrong, really wrong.'

Typically, the therapist would listen until my trains of thought ran out of steam. In fact, any time I'd asked questions previously in the hope of starting a conversation, I'd been met with that friendly silence therapists excel at, a tube down the gullet to syphon your cloudy emotional tank. I'd rambled about having threesomes, suicidal ideation, grief induced adjustment disorder, debilitating panic attacks ... and now, a walk along St Kilda beach with my kids, partners and five melting choc-tops.

'I'm so sorry,' she said, leaning forward in her chair, brow knitted.

'No, that's fine,' I said from the sofa, eager to assume all blame, keep the peace and stress about it later. And it *was* fine, I thought – it's OK to have an opinion.

After a few more seconds of silence, she said: 'That was really unprofessional of me, I'm so sorry, I don't know what came over me.'

'No, really, it's fine,' I said again.

We – I – spoke about other things for the rest of our hour together and I left thanking her, wishing her well and confirming I'd be back next week. But as the following Friday approached, I felt awkward and sent a note to say I wouldn't be able to make it, after which I never returned.

It's hardly scientific but I get the sense that people can really hate it when you mess openly and unapologetically with the nuclear model.

Recently, a woman got in touch with me on Facebook. She'd had a few drinks, she wrote, and thought 'what the hell, I should write to you' … She wanted to tell me she'd suggested and read *Poly* with her book club in South Australia and it had elicited 'a very strong response' from everyone.

'Oh, thanks heaps for suggesting it to your club,' I messaged back the following morning. '*Very strong* sounds potentially great and potentially concerning.'

'It's quite a polarising topic,' she replied a few minutes later.

'Yeah,' I wrote, getting out of bed, yawning. 'Nonmonogamy brings out really strong feelings and thoughts in people, especially when there are kids to consider.'

And that, I thought, was that. I was emptying cereal into bowls for my kids a short time later when my phone pinged again: 'Yes, it was the fact they were parents that really threw a spanner in the works.'

Such concerns can spill over into other ones too. A number of reviews of *Poly* brought up the drug use of the parents, Sarah and Chris, which comprises taking MDMA a couple of times while out dancing (their first nights out together without children in nearly a decade) and smoking a handful of joints in their back garden over the course of several months, while the kids are sleeping or staying with their grandparents.

In terms of substance abuse, it's not *Trainspotting*, and no greater than the recreational drug use of many perfectly capable parents of young children. But I've seen Sarah and Chris described as 'drug-addled', even 'drug addicts', their relationship and recreational choices combining, warping and expanding like a bad trip, man.

Don't get me wrong. I'm OK with the idea of being protective of children in novels. I deplore how Oliver Twist is treated by Bill Sikes, worry for little Lucy and her siblings in *The Lion, The Witch and The Wardrobe*.

Even though I'm sceptical, I don't ultimately mind if some readers think Sarah and Chris Flood are bad parents. But that same nonchalance evaporates quickly whenever I sense negative judgement of my real-life parenting with my real-life children.

I bring this up with Simon Copland while we're discussing his relationship with his two male partners. 'I think I probably face fewer challenges being in a poly relationship as a gay man compared to someone like you,' he says. 'Particularly because you have kids. That norm is so valorised that it must be quite challenging for a lot of people who are in a situation like yours.'

I came clean with my sons when they were five and seven. It was sooner than I'd expected but consistent with my decision not to lie to them about anything unless I had to for their safety (or when everyone warned me not to tell who really ate the carrots and drank the glass of milk on our kitchen table).

They'd overheard one of Kate's neighbours referring to me as Kate's boyfriend and asked the obvious question as I was driving them both home from her house:

'Is Kate your ... girlfriend?' my youngest asked.

'Yes, she is,' I said.

'Ah, because she's a girl and she's your friend,' my older son suggested.

'Well, no, it's more like I'm her boyfriend and she's my girlfriend,' I said. 'Mummy also has a boyfriend at the moment but Mummy and Daddy are married and love each other too. And, of course, we love you two more than anything else in the world. Does that make sense? Do you have any questions?'

I drove on in silence to give them a few minutes to process – they were pre-sexual at the time, so I couldn't explain adult relationships in those terms. I looked in the mirror once or twice, pulled funny faces. They smiled back, seemed tired but relaxed.

'I have a question,' my eldest said eventually. 'Can we have fish and chips for dinner tonight?'

'I have friends in poly relationships who have kids,' Simon says. 'There's always this fear from other people that kids won't understand. But, you know, my niece and nephew are eight and six and they don't have a problem with it. They're just like, "It's Uncle Simon and Uncle James and Uncle Martyn". Kids have no difficulty comprehending that.'

The 'compulsory sexuality' Angela Chen writes about in the book *Ace* is adapted from the American poet and writer Adrienne Rich's 1980 essay *Compulsory Heterosexuality and Lesbian Existence*, which theorised that women are conditioned to see relationships with men as the default, and therefore devalue relationships with other women. It doesn't need to be communicated to anyone in bright flashing lights that heterosexuality is somehow better than lesbianism, the argument goes – it just has to exist and be treated as the norm. Could it be, even as our stats tell a different story, we're still at the mercy of the 'compulsory nuclear family'?

'Where there are multiple partners, those extra parental figures are often a positive in kids' lives rather than a confusing negative,' Simon says. 'It's very strange that we think kids can only have two loving adult figures in a parental role when more adults in their lives is a really good thing. We all have our flaws and we all have our problems, so different forces and influences can actually be helpful. That's how our society worked for long periods and there are still communities out there that live like that.'

To take just one opposing view, Dr Karen Ruskin, in a 2013 article, wrote that polyamorous parenthood is 'less than ideal with potentially traumatic effects' for children.

> These children are not receiving more love living in a home environment of parents who live a life of polyamory. They are receiving more loss, and thus either go through life mourning and grieving, or they learn to shut themselves off to love knowing it will end once a breakup occurs – that is out of their control.

> Love pulled out from under the rug, any day any time is not a healthy way for a child to live. Thus, when their parent argues with one of their lovers, the child may fear the end is near, never knowing when this person they love and [who] loves them will no longer exist in their life. Children living in this existence may have a hard time giving and receiving love, as the effects of this lifestyle.[71]

Scary, right? Who wants to traumatise their kids? The implication in arguments of this sort seems to be that nonmonogamous parents are either negligent or don't care that they're causing their kids trauma, and sadly, that's almost certainly true in some cases. Percentage-wise, I can only imagine there are as many good, bad and indifferent nonmonogamous parents and guardians as there are monogamous ones.

Arguments, break-ups, grief and loss are part of being alive – as are, in the best cases, solid love and support networks to help kids grow up and prosper in the face of those realities.

The 2013 study *Children in Polyamorous Families: A First Empirical Look found* that children raised by parents with multiple partners 'can benefit from having multiple loving parents who can offer not only more quality time, but a greater range of interests and energy levels to match the child's own unique and growing personality.'[72]

Personally, I doubt the benefits of having more than two parental figures would ever automatically outweigh those of having one or two, and vice versa. It all comes down to people, the majority of whom, in my experience, are doing what they can to be decent humans who don't let themselves and their loved ones down too often.

'We've privatised it so that only two people can ever be responsible for the child, and maybe a grandparent or two if they're around,' Simon says. 'That puts a lot of strain on the parents but it can also really limit the opportunities the children have for adult role models who can love them and care for them and teach them things. You get your parents, your grandparents, and your teachers to an extent, which is a very narrow view of what children may want and need.'

○○○

In *Invented Lives* and elsewhere, Andrea Goldsmith writes about marriages and families that are seemingly unconventional, but says now, 'I don't know how unconventional they really are'.

Growing up, the nuclear family she belonged to held firm, more or less, without too much harmful radiation. 'I mean, my mother had an affair for 20 years,' she says. 'My father was very unhappy about that, but I expect he did what men did in those days and took a few excursions out from the marriage himself. What I have discovered since becoming an adult and talking to other people is the amazing number of people my age, with parents who were born in the 1920s, whose mothers had a long affair and the marriage stayed together. Appearances were maintained even though, in the case of my parents, all their friends knew what was going on.'

○ ○ ○

Rob McDonald always knew he wanted children. 'I never equated being gay with being sterile, as some people bizarrely do without thinking,' he says. 'That's the sort of message you were always shown or told.'

He co-parents his two daughters with two mums who were previously in a relationship with each other.

'I'd been sharing a house with one of the mums but neither of us had ever discussed parenting,' he says. 'Then this one time, at a dinner party, someone asked us, "What would you call your first child?", and we both said "Jack" at the same time. It made the hairs on the back of our necks stand on end.

'We avoided each other in the house for the next 24 hours, and when we eventually spoke, we were like, "Something's going on here". We discussed the fact we're both from families of four and discovered we both had the same aspirational parenting values. They got their partner involved in the conversation and it was the same thing – we all had similar ideas about parenting.

'We brought our families on board from the start and accessed Maybe Baby, a group in Melbourne set up to help queers who wanted to form a family in whatever shape that might be. We got some DIY advice from people who had been through it before.

'This was during the John Howard years, when they were putting through the amendment to the Marriage Act to prevent same-sex marriages, so it almost felt like an act of rebellion to be doing home insemination, not that we had our kids as any kind of protest.'

And it worked. Before long a baby was baking, and then – sooner than expected – another. 'We thought it might take 18 months for the second mum to get pregnant, but it happened nearly straight away,' Rob says. 'So our two daughters are very close in age, which has been fantastic. I mean, obviously it's a lot of work ...'

Now teenagers, Rob's daughters spend time between their parents' three houses, where there is consistency and broad agreement on parenting values.

'Like any family, there are ups and downs and it's certainly involved a lot of negotiating and compromising between the three of us as parents,' Rob says. 'But if we're arguing it's usually because we want to spend more time with the kids, which in a way is nice.'

'Because it's a different structure to the one we were raised with, we used to take the kids every six months to meet with a child psychologist. They're resilient, which is no surprise to anyone, but they're also doing really well at school and in their friendships – they're just amazing kids.'

Both children experienced homophobia at their previous school which, while not necessarily directed at them, had an impact on the whole family. 'It's been interesting seeing that through my daughters' eyes,' Rob says. 'You hear the racial slurs in the playground, homophobic slurs, these boys calling girls "bitches" and thinking it's funny. It's still being normalised for young boys to continue with this kind of behaviour, and then it gets more and more robust. Of course, there are some great boys out there who are allies and who don't devolve into that.'

When my youngest son was being bullied, I distinctly remember wanting to hurt the boy who was doing it. We contacted the school and spoke to the teacher: the bullying continued. My son came home with bruises. We spoke to the teacher again. He came home with scrapes. In the end, we tried a two-pronged response. I taught my son to raise his hand in a stop sign and shout 'LEAVE ME ALONE, LOSER' at the top of his lungs any time the boy came near him, and I also (by chance) happened to see the boy one morning during school drop-off. He ran across the front oval to my son, probably to thump him, at which point I got to my knees, gave him a death stare and said: 'Your fingers will turn into parsnips if you ever touch my son again, do you understand?'

He did.

'One of the conversations I've been having with my kids is the difference between polite and respectful,' Rob says. 'Particularly when it comes to male violence, because I don't want them being polite to some absolute arsehole of a guy who's actually a threat. It's about being respectful to someone until they don't give you respect. As a parent, you want your kids to have less baggage than you had and hopefully the cycle of abuse will get broken.'

The 'post-homophobic' world of Rob's novels *The Nancys* and *Nancy Business* was inspired in part by the heartbreaking story in 2014 of an 11-year-old American boy called Michael Morones who attempted suicide and lived out the remainder of his life in a persistent vegetative state after being relentlessly bullied for, among other things, loving My Little Pony. He died seven years later, in 2021.

'I wanted to explore this idea of a world where homophobia no longer existed,' Rob says. 'I really wanted to take the non-queer reader into the story, to show them what life is like for me. If you take away the abuse and fear of being bashed, this is the world we inhabit and it's fucking awesome. We have these wonderful found families, with love and respect in this very close-knit way. You might have a grandmother figure or older-sister figure. There's a family bond where you're honest with each other and vulnerable and enjoy spending time together. Of course, there are arguments, just as there should be with any relationship that's growing – because that's part of being in a family too.'

○ ○ ◡

One of the reasons I was stressed about running late to meet Filip Vukašin on the day of our interview was that I knew he was on a tight schedule. For us to chat face-to-face, he's had to arrange a babysitter for his six-month-old twin girls and two-year-old son.

'When I first met Matt, I told him I saw kids in my future, but he had never considered it,' Filip says. 'He's six years older than me so maybe he just thought it wasn't going to happen.'

'The year we were getting married we decided to start the ball rolling. We looked at all the options and for a whole manner of reasons decided on surrogacy.'

They sought advice from friends who had gone through a similar process, contacted some agencies overseas, and eventually – after numerous video calls – settled on an agency in the States. 'It's like online dating,' Filip says. 'You answer lots of questions and upload photos of yourself. The agent then makes a profile for you and shares it with the surrogates. You get to see the surrogates' profiles too, so you can find out how many kids they have, what languages they speak, their job, all of that. You pick someone you like, but they have to pick you too for it to be a match.'

Before long, he says, they were having an interview with Jennifer, their first surrogate. 'We were like "Oh my god, this is happening,"' he says. 'We spoke to Jennifer, then we spoke to our egg donor, Brooke. We'd decided that we wanted to have a relationship with our egg donor so that our kids would know who they were too.'

They flew to America, met both women, and within six months had an embryo transfer. 'The first go didn't work but the second did,' Filip says. 'We got to America about three weeks before our son was born. The agents asked if we were planning to do it again and said we could meet another surrogate while we were there because Jennifer was going to retire.'

'We met another surrogate called Karla, and we already had embryos stored, so we got things moving even before our son was born. And then the embryo split, and we ended up with twins.'

Filip's laughter seems warm and genuine, not maniacal and stressed as you might expect with this turn of events. Despite Karla's pregnancy coinciding with the worst of the pandemic-related travel restrictions in 2020 and 2021, they made it back to the States just in time for the twins' birth.

'Matt told them I was a doctor, so I got to help the obstetrician deliver the babies,' he says. 'We've got really great relationships with both surrogates and our egg donor. We feel lucky we were there for the delivery with Jennifer and her husband. Brooke, our egg donor, has met all the kids, and Karla too. We feel like we've got a real family over there. We send them photos, they send us photos. It's so cool.'

Given they live in an ostensibly progressive inner-city Melbourne suburb, I'm guessing Matt and Filip don't get the same raised eyebrows they might if they lived in more conservative parts of the country, but they still must attract attention, right?

'Literally everyone is looking at us when the five of us are out together,' Filip says. 'Two guys with beards and three tiny kids – everyone stares, but I think that's because it's so intriguing, and we don't get offended by it at all.'

They get stopped, he says, all the time. 'People want to know where the kids are from, whether they're from Matt or me, whose sperm we used, and we're totally open about it. We decided before our son was born that we weren't going to have any secrets about who's from who genetically ... I mean, we don't go through every detail with randoms necessarily, but the more we share our story, the more we think it will help other people.'

He recalls one time in the States when Matt was flummoxed by the shocked reaction of two women in a shop when he said their son had two dads and no mum.

'That led us to conversation where we were both, like, "Actually, it's not true that he doesn't have a mother – he has two". And so that's what we say now: he's got a tummy-mummy and an egg-mummy.

'We've been in the park before and other kids have come across to us and said, "Where's their mummy?" When we say, "They've got two daddies and two mummies" they're like "Whoaaaaa ..."'

12
Holding up a mirror

In commending the Same-Sex Marriage Bill to Parliament after the Australian Marriage Law Postal Survey in 2017, then-Prime Minister Malcolm Turnbull said the following:

> The Australian people have said 'yes' to marriage equality, 'yes' to fairness, 'yes' to commitment, 'yes' to love. The time has now come to make that equality a reality.

> Now this is momentous social reform and the road to this day has been long and arduous. It's littered with injustice dealt out to men and women who dared to confess their love.

> Not so long ago, homosexuality was a crime in this country. [...] The message today to every gay person in this nation is clear: We love you. We respect you.[73]

Despite the voluntary nature of the survey, nearly 80 per cent of the electorate – 12,727,920 people – responded to the question: 'Should the law be changed to allow same-sex couples to marry?'

Some 7,817,247 (61.6 per cent of the vote) people said it should, while 4,873,987 (38.4 per cent) said it shouldn't.

In his speech, Turnbull reminded everyone he was the first prime minister of Australia to have 'unequivocally and consistently' supported legalising same-sex marriage. It would 'be forever to the credit' of his government, he added, that this 'momentous social change' occurred under the Liberal–National Coalition.

Leaving aside the fact it was his Liberal predecessor John Howard who, in 2004, changed the law to block same-sex marriages, the 2017 re-set *was* – and continuous to be – momentous.

Turnbull, a moderate Liberal and vocal supporter of marriage equality, clearly played a significant role, as did the first openly gay Liberal Party backbencher Senator Dean Smith, who introduced the private member's bill calling for marriage to once again be defined as a 'union of two people to the exclusion of all others' rather than a 'union of a man and woman'.

As to why this would come to pass under a right-leaning Coalition government after 22 unsuccessful attempts to amend the Act in the preceding 13 years, Turnbull's speech offers some clues:

> *If consulted by friends about marital dramas, I always encourage the singles to marry, the married to stick together, the neglectful and wayward to renew their loving commitment, and the wrong to forgive. [...] Are not gay people who seek the right to marry, to formalise their commitment to each other, holding up a mirror to heterosexuals who regrettably, in my view at least, are marrying less frequently and divorcing more often?*

Later in that same speech, echoing the rationale of former Conservative UK Prime Minister David Cameron, who presided over same-sex marriage legislation in 2014, he added:

> Society is stronger when we make vows to each other and support each other. So, I don't support gay marriage despite being a Conservative. I support gay marriage because I'm a Conservative.

Omar Sakr's view that many of the narratives supporting same-sex marriage were 'inherently conservative' comes to mind, as do the various ways the victory was greeted at the time. If you were out and about on that Wednesday evening, 15 November 2017, there's a good chance you saw people – and potentially lots of people – celebrating in ways that rarely happen outside of sporting victories or the end of wars.

In Melbourne, I remember getting rained on a lot and being squished among hundreds of people in the CBD as live music played and bodies danced, trying to tell my largely disinterested kids (they were hungry and wet) that this was history in the making. They liked the rainbow flags, though. What had been a bruising campaign had come to an end with equality as the clear winner.

None of the people I've talked to for this book said they thought it was bad that the vote came back in favour of same-sex marriage – for many, if nothing else, it was a relief. But very few talked about it with unqualified enthusiasm either.

Dr Jessica Kean sees the discourse leading up to and surrounding the same-sex marriage amendment through the broader lens of 'conditions of acceptance for gay folk'.

'It's this idea of parents saying it's OK that you're gay but it being conditional on being a certain kind of gay person,' she says. 'So, you know, I have friends whose parents have been like, "Thank god you're not one of those really butch lesbians," or others who are like, "It's OK, you can still get married", or "It's OK, you can still have children". It's about being able to fulfill a heteronormative vision of what it means to have a life and family and meaningful relationships. This is still the condition on which the acceptance of queer people hinges.'

In the case of marriage, it's also a reflection of what a number of queer people wanted to do. Around 4.6 per cent of marriages in Australia since 1 January 2018 have been same-sex – with 2,757 male and 3,781 female unions taking place in the first year it was legal.

'It's interesting because, I mean, there are lots of queer people for whom that is actually the dream,' Jessica says. 'But there are also big parts of queer communities who don't see that as the ideal. For lots of people, some of the proudest moments of queer culture are about shaking up those norms or having the freedom to live outside of them. I think that shows you exactly how limited the same-sex marriage victory has been for queer people. It's not very queer, actually – it's a conditional acceptance.

'When the amendment got up, I remember thinking "Oh shit, am I going to be subjected to the same pressure that straight people have always been under – you know, "time's ticking" … I'd been blissfully exempt from that particular life horizon for so long and had avoided being pushed by family in that direction. And, I mean, it still hasn't happened, my family know me better, but I do remember thinking, "Oh god, now queers are going to have to deal with that too".'

○ ○ ○

Lest it be popularly construed (rightly) as legislation that would and could pass only with the support of the Labor shadow government, Liberal Attorney General George Brandis said in 2017 that the amendment to the Marriage Act would 'stand as one of the signature achievements' of the Turnbull government and become its 'imperishable legacy':

> I predict that […] this decision by the Australian people, enabled by their government and enacted by their Parliament, will come to be seen as one of those occasional shining moments which stand out in our nation's history, about which people will still speak with admiration in decades, indeed in centuries to come; one of those breakthroughs which have, as the wheel of history turns, defined us as a people.[74]

Of course, it's the bread and butter of politics to take credit for events that play well with the electorate while slamming your opponents for those that don't, but the grandeur and sentiment of Brandis's speech felt – and still feels – right for the moment. Yes, it big-upped Australia as a nation but what were so many of us doing that November night in 2017 if not waving (rainbow) flags for Australia and how it could now see itself?

Peter Polites, when we chat, talks about 'homonationalism' – a term coined by the US-based philosopher and queer theorist Jasbir K. Puar in her 2007 book *Terrorist Assemblages: Homonationalism in Queer Times*. Among other things, the term is used to describe the ways nationalists in the US and elsewhere champion certain LGBTQIA+ rights in return for the complicity of LGBTQIA+ people within a broader nationalist agenda – a type of virtue signalling and point-scoring on an international level.

In developing the concept, Puar wrote mainly about the US war on terror where, following the Twin Towers attacks in 2001, the US positioned itself as LGBT-friendly to differentiate itself from supposedly homophobic Muslim nations – the rough shorthand being: 'We are modern – they are not'.

Such a strategy involves only a slight update to, and reworking of, an age-old practice. Colonisation has long relied on painting the colonised as barbarians and the colonisers as benevolent bringers of light, even though 'civilisation' tends to deliver mass death and suffering.

In the twentieth century alone, it's been posited that around 50 million people died directly through the impacts of colonial occupation.[75] One estimate suggests that, in the 23 years from 1885 to 1908, Belgium's occupation of Congo killed ten million people.[76]

A 2019 study published in the Quaternary Science Reviews theorised that the arrival of Europeans to the Americas in 1492 caused the death (by 1600) of 90 per cent of the Indigenous population – nearly 56 million people – the deaths occurring on such a large and rapid scale that atmospheric CO_2 plummeted, triggering the Little Ice Age.[77]

As Kurt Vonnegut might have glumly put it: So it goes.

Taking the most conservative projections of the Indigenous population at the time of European arrival in 1788, the Aboriginal History Journal estimates that more than 80 per cent of Australia's original inhabitants died as a direct result of colonisation.[78] This, too, is our 'imperishable legacy' at a local and global level.

All of which is to say that 'progressive' moves by governments and their societies aren't always what they're cracked up to be, even when they support steps in the right direction.

'We saw a similar thing when Western governments were trying to make it palatable to invade Afghanistan,' Peter says. 'The American government was saying to the Democrats, "We've got to go in there and free the women".'

The idea of homonationalism is integral to Peter's novel The Pillars, in which the narrator Pano pretends to be a gay Albanian Muslim as part of a plan to prevent a mosque being built in his Western Sydney neighbourhood. The true motivation is Pano's landlord/lover's concerns about property prices falling if the mosque gets built, the solution for which – he thinks – is to play up 'old-world tribal tensions' and stop the development in its tracks.

'Pano uses the homophobia that's apparently inherent in Islam, which is obviously not true, as a weapon of capitalism,' Peter says. 'For me, it was a comment about the fact that fags can be agents of conservatism for a national or capitalist dynamic. That was a big part of The Pillars. Some ideologies fit perfectly within the blanket of capitalist conservatism, and some don't.'

He cites the Safe Schools program, a group of Australian organisations with a mission to create inclusive schools for same-sex attracted, gender diverse and intersex young people and their families.

Introduced in Victoria in 2010 and expanded nationally in 2013 with bipartisan support and $8 million federal funding, the program was reviewed in 2016 under the Coalition government, and federal funding was halted the following year. To give an idea of the tenor of commentary at the time, the New South Wales iteration of the program was described by former prime minister Tony Abbott – whose government initiated Safe Schools nationally – as 'a social engineering program dressed up as anti-bullying'.[79]

The Democratic Labour Party – which was 'born out of the need to protect Australians from the increasing presence of communist influence' – professed a similar view:

> It's advertised as an anti-bullying program, but it has a far more sinister purpose. It is ideologically driven, teaching our children a contested and controversial form of gender ideology to further radical social and political agendas more than anything else. There is now increasing awareness that its ultimate purpose is the social re-engineering of children.[80]

In Victoria, meanwhile, where Safe Schools still operates, its website emphasises the voluntary nature of the program, whereby schools 'have the discretion to use as many or as few of the resources, training materials, and other support' as they see fit to 'help them prevent, and respond to, bullying and discrimination based on sexual orientation, gender identity or intersex status' and create an environment more attuned to 'preventing suicide and self-harm'.[81] If that's the social re-engineering of children we're talking about, sign me up – I'm all in.

'The Safe Schools debate was happening at the same time as the marriage equality debate but only one was successful,' Peter says. 'Why? Because marriage equality is an individualistic, small 'l' liberal campaign that conservatives left and right can get involved with.

'Continuing to back Safe Schools would essentially have been about structural reform. It would have been infinitely more beneficial to schools, infinitely more beneficial for queer and trans kids and for educating a bunch of people, but structural reforms are kind of impossible in our neoliberal society.'

○ ○ ○

'We were told that we weren't allowed to display any "Yes" campaign material at the school I was teaching at unless it was approved by the education union,' Roz Bellamy remembers. 'But the students were bringing it up and wanted to talk about it. So there was this strange situation where the teachers, on the whole, were quite supportive of having those discussions and airing those views but the school itself wasn't.'

It would have been a fair assumption at the time that Roz would be backing the Yes vote. Roz and their wife had already committed to each other through a legal commitment ceremony in 2013 in the UK, and later converted that to marriage when the law allowed for it in Britain. 'We counted each one as getting married,' they say.

The hat-trick, though, remained elusive. 'We thought about getting married again in Australia, when it became legal, but then found out we couldn't because we'd already married overseas.'

Would Andrea Goldsmith have married her partner, Dot, had it been possible at the time?

'Dot always said if she could marry me, she would,' Andrea says. 'But I always said, "Over my dead body".

'I'm of an age where marriage was on the nose. The whole business of all those lesbians and gay men fighting to get the right to marry … I was thinking "God, don't you have more ambition than that?" At the same time, of course I voted in favour. Of course. But I did sort of think, "Why would you want to replicate a system that's been so damaging to you?"'

○ ○ ○

Does Christos Tsiolkas see the same-sex marriage victory as a win for conservative values, a watershed moment for Australia, a sign of social progress, or a mix of all those things?

'Actually, same-sex marriage was never on my radar,' he says. 'When the debate first started, I remember thinking it was a really negative thing, because it was aping that heteronormative idea.

'I don't see it that way now. I see it as progressive in the sense that it speaks to a greater acceptance of different sexualities, which is a good thing.

'The conservative element is still there, though. People have so many different ways of forming relationships, so why are we prioritising this one?

'But on the day of the postal vote result it was just a relief because it would have been a nightmare if it went the other way.'

So, a watershed moment, then?

'It wasn't a watershed moment for me personally,' he says, 'but I think it was a really important moment politically in the history of the country.

'For me, that's also an indication of my age. There has to be a time where you just go, "I'm an older man – I'm not one of the young ones". And that's fine. I've been active politically since I was 16 but I never saw the same-sex marriage debate coming – it blindsided me.

'I understand the celebration of relationships. When Wayne and I turned 40, and had already been together for 21 years, we had a big party at our place with both of our families and friends. That was one of the loveliest nights of my life. I don't really need marriage.'

○○○

I know from reading *Unrequited Love*, Dennis Altman's memoir and diary covering the years 2016 to 2018, that he was both supportive and questioning of the issue of same-sex marriage. In his diary entry for 15 November, 2017, the day the postal vote result was announced, he wrote:

> Today felt like a major milestone, but I don't think the zeitgeist shifted, rather that several decades of slow shifts towards greater acceptance came together, and most Australians recognised this.[82]

Here's what he says about it now:

'Well, I think a lot of us couldn't get very excited about marriage as the ultimate goal. There were many people who felt the emphasis on marriage as somehow the most important achievement for the movement was short-sighted.

'I think it's important, though, to recognise what happened in Australia, which is different to what necessarily happened elsewhere. When it became a postal vote, it was a vote about much more than marriage – it became a vote about acceptance. And in that sense, it was enormously important. Although we got there through the determination of conservatives to try to delay same-sex marriage for as long as possible, I think the outcome was far better than anything we could have expected.'

Holden Sheppard likewise sees the same-sex marriage outcome as a more-than-half-full glass. 'A lot of activists will say things are just as bad as they've ever been for gay and lesbian people, and I'm like, "You know, we can fundamentally prove they're not". The fact that two-thirds of Australians voted for us to get married tells us that.

'After the results were announced, I remember someone saying, 'I feel terrible because I'm walking down the street thinking about the one-in-three people who didn't want me to get married". Meanwhile,

I was like, "I feel awesome because two out of every three people are OK with me getting married. And of the one in three who voted "no", they might not necessarily be angry homophobes. They might be like, "Well, I'm OK with it, but I don't know if they should call it marriage".' We've come a long way from the '70s and '80s.'

○○○

The fact the vote resulted in a victory for the Yes campaign was one thing; the fact it could just as easily have been a win for the No side is quite another.

'It should never have gone to a postal vote,' Rob McDonald says. 'The $80.5 million it cost could have been put into aged care or mental health, and parliament should have just done its job.'

'The silver lining was that it put paid to the hateful propaganda that said the majority of people didn't want same-sex marriage to be allowed.

'Another positive through the debate was that the non-queer Australian public got to hear a lot of queer voices ... I mean, they heard a lot of hate too, but they got to see and hear a lot of queer people talking in a transparent and open way. Sadly, it was also a horrible, triggering time.'

Unlike me, Rob didn't find himself being slapped repeatedly in the face with rainbow flags in Melbourne's CBD.

'I know there were people out celebrating when the result came through but, honestly, I just went and hid in my bedroom,' he says. 'Our family had got together, the parents and kids, to watch the results, and I was sitting there with my daughters thinking, "If this is a No result, how am I going to explain it to them?"

OOO

When I ask Chris Cheers whether the marriage victory was a step forward for society, he visibly blanches. 'When I hear that question, it's very hard for me as a psychologist and a queer person to not immediately focus on the devastating impacts to mental health and wellbeing the postal vote had,' he says.

'It takes me back to a period of almost ten years where it was put out there for other people to decide whether my clients, my friends, my partners and me were valid or not.

'We became political, as if we were an issue rather than people. From all the issues affecting everyone, this was the one that had to go across the whole of Australia for everyone to decide. Many people are still working through the trauma of that period.'

And, of course, new traumas happen daily, over and above those being slowly processed. 'Trans people – including kids – are now being used politically in the way that gay and lesbian people were,' Chris says. 'Their rights and need to be protected are being threatened for the sake of politics.

'The same-sex marriage decision in the end, though it caused so much pain and devastation for mental health, led to progress for our rights. But I say "our" with the knowledge I'm just talking about same-sex attracted people and their right to marry. For some parts of the population, that's seen almost as if it ended homophobia but that's obviously not true. It also had nothing to do with progress in the trans or gender-diverse space.

'When it comes to intersex, to trans, to gender-diverse, to other populations who are in far more need in many ways for their rights to be protected, it certainly doesn't feel like progress. If anything, it feels like they've been left behind.'

As Australian historian Yves Rees puts it in their 2021 memoir *All About Yves*, aside from the systemic legal and political obstacles facing trans people, there's no shortage of everyday bigotry, fear and ignorance:

> TERFS [trans-exclusionary radical feminists] and other transphobes like to blame the increased incidence of transness on 'social contagion' or 'peer pressure'. But the truth is much more banal. It's simply that, thanks to increased trans visibility and the ubiquity of the internet, more people now have opportunity to put words to the gender trouble that's haunted us for so long. Transness isn't infection or trend; it's a new name for an old feeling – a feeling that's deeply human and remarkably common.[83]

Chris would like to see greater positive momentum building. 'I do hope the same amount of activism and energy and support that was garnered during the marriage equality campaign leads to those same people coming out now at rallies and online to support trans and gender-diverse kids, young people and adults.'

13
Things fall apart

Looking back, I can see it's been years since my marriage started coming apart, but the seams gave way completely a couple of years ago – a popping sound, a hiss of fabric, the awareness that a patch wouldn't work this time.

After facing up to reality, the worst part for me was the prospect of telling our kids. It's not what I wanted for them and, to be honest, that was all that was keeping things together by the end, the last root filament holding onto a tooth as it wiggles in the gum.

Jess and I thought we should wait until I'd found a new place to live before telling our boys, and I agreed. And soon enough, with Kate, that place was found.

I won't go into too much detail about the conversation Jess and I had with the kids on our bed that Saturday morning because it would feel like a breach of their privacy and ours but there was a gasp from one of my sons I'll never forget, an involuntary 'oh no' that breaks my heart to remember. If you ever want to feel deep guilt, anger, sadness and hopelessness simultaneously, disappointing your kids in this way is a good place to start.

We showed them real-estate photos of the house I'd be moving into, a rental that was way bigger than the one we were currently in, and one of my kids asked mainly about that: could he use the en-suite bathroom sometimes, even though it was in my bedroom? Did all the rooms have plug sockets? The floor plan said there was an outdoor spa – was there really an outdoor spa? (No, sadly, there wasn't).

Though numbing, I at least had the sense that the moment I'd been dreading for so long had passed. We went out together with our dog that afternoon – a mum, dad and their two sons. We walked along the flooded Merri Creek, throwing sticks for the dog, laughing, chatting, a nuclear unit rendered radioactively unstable but, to anyone who might be watching, still intact.

Like me, Jess had to find a new place to stay but was struggling to find something suitable. A few weeks before my move date, which fell mercifully between Melbourne's stay-at-home orders, Kate suggested Jess stay with us at our new place until she found somewhere – a proposal that was well received by everyone.

Our all-moving-in-together came a couple of weeks before yet another protracted lockdown in which the children had to be homeschooled, everyone had to work at home and the permitted reasons to go further than the garden fence didn't include getting a break from the surprisingly minor but still cumulative tension of three adults, two children, two cats, one dog and twenty-six house plants breathing the same oxygen for 24 hours a day, seven days a week, for months on end.

In reality, then, the census response that would have most accurately represented our true situation on the evening of August 10, 2021 would have been me and my:

☐ Spouse (separated but under the same roof), partner and two children.

A couple of people have shaken their heads in wonder when they hear we endured lockdown together but, really, it was the most relaxed I'd been since early 2016. Instead of waking up at Kate's feeling anxious and guilty that I wasn't with my kids, or being with Jess and the kids feeling anxious and guilty that I wasn't with Kate, I was able to just be.

I could wake up without sensing I'd started the day in debt. I didn't have to run myself ragged all the time trying to demonstrate my love for everyone but myself. After years of that, it was a relief to know the people I cared most about were all under the same roof, that we could have breakfast, lunch and dinner together – or not, depending on everyone's mood and daily preferences. Despite the lack of exercise and a prolonged existential dread that disease and/or environmental collapse would kill us far sooner than we'd like, it was the best time, really – an arrangement I'd been proposing to both partners, with no luck, for ages.

Now that we're living in separate places, it's become more obvious that Jess and I still are, and will continue to be, a family unit, even if we're scattered like Lego pieces. We live at different addresses in the same suburb and have adjusted to the frustrations and forgotten socks of the kids swapping houses week to week, all the while doing what we can to make sure their days are filled with laughter, that they feel loved and safe. It's clear Jess and I will remain in each other's lives. If separating was like having our legs untied after a seemingly endless three-legged race, post-separation has seen our ankles re-tied with a new, and gentler, knot.

Splitting up hurts, that much is obvious, and having children's wellbeing to contend with doesn't lighten the load. There's nothing unique in the type of pain I've felt – you've felt it too, it's as much yours as it is mine. But the dynamic in and around this break-up has differentiated it from any I've had in the past.

If it's true that it takes half the length of a relationship to recover once it ends, Jess and I can look forward to a full decade of mourning. But I'm also more than six years into another relationship with a woman I love, the second-longest romantic pairing of my life and hers. There aren't many examples to follow in that situation.

From books, films, songs, theatre, visual art and my own life experience, I know I'm supposed to get drunk and have some rebound sex, get a new hairstyle, bob up and down between elation and despair, break things, feel lonely, reconnect with estranged friends, take up new hobbies and eventually – if the stars align – start seeing someone new.

The pros of already having that other person in my life are self-evident: I'm being supported, I'm in love, my kids don't need to be introduced to a new partner because they've known Kate for most of their lives. But some cons exist too. There's been a confusing invisibility to the end of my marriage, a lack of ceremony around this 20-year relationship dying. I can't think of any close friends or family who've got in touch to say they're sorry about it ending, partially because I'm good at hiding from prospective pity but mostly, I think, because I'm in another relationship. A similar thing happened when Kate and I split up temporarily a couple of years into our time together – very few people, even those we'd socialised with regularly since we started seeing each other, acknowledged the break-up with me. Wasn't I still married? Yeah … So what was I worried about? The rites of passage for the end of relationships, like so many other rites, are designed for monogamy. If Jess was one arm and Kate the other, people can only see the one that wasn't lopped off.

○ ○ ○

Dealing with the death or transmogrification of one relationship within a broader romantic ecosystem isn't easy. When we speak, Chris Cheers has been with one partner for five years, the other for two.

When he and Nic met Joel, all three started dating as a thruple. About a year later, the thruple ended, with Chris and Nic remaining a couple, and then Chris and Joel getting back together. In poly terms, this 'vee' relationship (as in, the letter V) sees Chris as the 'pivot', or the pointy bit of the V, dating Nic and Joel separately. Nic and Joel, meanwhile, are now 'metamours', which sounds like something from the court of Louis XVII, the kind of term that should come with white face powder and a fan, but just means a partner's partner with whom you're not romantically involved. Getting to that stage for Chris, Nic and Joel has involved – how could it not? – a lot of manoeuvring.

'It was a complex and challenging process,' Chris says.

As with nearly every other facet of consensual nonmonogamy, communication to the point of over-communication has been key.

'We've been through therapy to help the process and I've been doing a lot of reading,' Chris says. 'We've been talking a lot. But it would be fair to say it's been really challenging, especially on my Nic. He's had to go through a break-up, which is already challenging, but even more so because it's a break-up where his ex is also dating his partner.'

I'm reminded of the readers' comment section on Simon Copland's 2015 article for *The Guardian*, 'Dating two people at once: why I'm polyamorous and proud', summed up most succinctly in a response from a reader called CCoasty:

'… [it's] too difficult in my opinion, a couple is hard work enough in my book.'[84]

With hard work comes benefits, though, as Chris can confirm. 'Tom and I were quite dependent on each other,' he says. 'We started living together very quickly after we started seeing each other, our friends were each other's friends. I think my second partner represented a threat to that. But it also meant my longer-term partner had to start to think about what he wanted in his life, because I wanted this other space outside of our relationship.

'At the time it was really difficult, especially because we navigated this during lockdown, but we've said from the beginning that we know it will be better for us long-term if we can work through this. For me, the idea of being together with someone forever is a ridiculous concept, and the only way we see that being even remotely possible is if we allow the space within our relationship for us both to have independence. We're much stronger now, much more open and genuine and honest with each other.'

○ ○ ○

Rochelle Siemienowicz's intimate relationship personnel increased from two to three eight years ago in ways her husband David wasn't expecting. She and David had been together for more than 20 years when she told him she'd been having an affair with Markus.

Contrary to the received wisdom that this could only mean the end of their marriage, they found ways to see the new reality as the death of what had been and the birth of something new. Like Rochelle, David now also has another long-term partner, Tash. Knowing them and having socialised together on many occasions, I struggle to think of many people who get along with each other better or who show each other such obvious respect and love.

'It's all very harmonious now,' Rochelle says. 'It was painful in the first year, with David having to come to terms with it all because it wasn't his choice to have this kind of relationship. It was thrust upon him and there was also a level of deception and devastation associated with that. So, yeah, there were emotional outbursts, there was screaming and yelling, but even from those early days there was a lot of goodwill and laughter.'

These days, Rochelle, David and their respective partners practise what Rochelle refers to as 'kitchen table polyamory'.

'We can all socialise together,' she says. 'We all know about each other's lives and what's going on. We're a family, even though we don't all co-habit or share finances. But there's definite longevity – we've written each other into our wills. There's an assumption that we'll continue together until death do us part, even though there are no new wedding rings.'

Rochelle's relationship with David's partner Tash, her metamour, has been mutually supportive and platonically loving since the start, which Rochelle says was never in doubt. 'David said he thought I'd really like Tash and I never thought there was a possibility I wouldn't,' she says. 'I just trusted him and, when I met her, I immediately trusted that she wasn't trying to steal him away. I don't think any of our relationships would work if we didn't genuinely like each other.'

Because of that, a lot hinged on the first meeting between David and Markus which, rather than guns at high noon, involved sharing a drink.

'David wanted to meet Markus on his own terms at a bar he chose, to have this man-on-man conversation,' Rochelle says.

'Some of Markus's friends were like, "Oh my god, you better be careful, this could come to blows". But I already knew these two men deeply and knew they were non-violent, goodhearted, intelligent, curious people who had so much in common. I trusted they would see eye-to-eye and they just really got on with each other.

'It wasn't the end of all the conflict, but it became an immediate sort of brotherhood almost. They met each other in a very emotionally vulnerable way – there wasn't that masculine competitive thing, even though there are moments even now when one or the other thinks something's unfair, and we have to talk and negotiate solutions everyone's happy with.'

There's also the issue of time, the bane of many a polyamorous set-up. Love might expand like a birthday sponge in the oven but time has to be divided and sub-divided with each new partner, a cutting of the cake that – if you're not careful – risks leaving you with little more than a sticky knife and plateful of crumby regrets.

But let's focus on the positives. In my own case, one of the highlights of polyamory has been the realisation that I exist as a romantic or potentially romantic prospect in different ways to different people – an epiphany that might seem trite and embarrassingly superficial, but not for me. For many years, I saw myself in large part through my wife's often squinting eyes. That wasn't her fault – I think I've always been like that. Had we split up before I fell in love with someone new, I'd probably have started seeing myself through that new person's eyes, then the next person's, and so on. Being in romantic relationships with more than one person concurrently has taught me emotionally what I've always assumed to be true intellectually: it's all subjective.

Elements of us that are a turn-off for one partner are a turn-on for someone else, not only *after* ending one relationship and refining (or hiding) those parts of ourselves but on the same day, even in the same moment. That's helped me to trust, laugh and cringe at myself a bit more. I know for certain now that one person's trash (me) is another person's treasure (me), even if most people see just another take-it-or-leave-it knick-knack in a suburban garage sale (also me).

'I love the fact that when you get really close to someone they shine back a different reflection and you're able to explore different facets of yourself,' Rochelle says.

She offers an example, one of many. 'David really doesn't dance very often – only when the music is in a very particular spectrum. In the past, we'd go to weddings and my girlfriends would say "Let's dance". I'd get up and dance awkwardly and David would say, "We don't dance". But then I met Markus, who loves to dance. He takes me out to see live music and I've experienced this freeing up of my body. Now I'm a dancer. I mean, I'm not a *dancer*, but I like to dance and don't feel like the most awkward person in the room now because I do it so often.'

○ ○ ○

Some endings are more permanent than others, of course, and – because of the people involved – more public.

The passing in 2012 of Dennis Altman's partner of 22 years, Anthony Smith, made national news. Among other significant achievements, Anthony had been Principal Researcher at La Trobe University's Australian Centre for Research in Sex, Health and Society, and presided over Australia's largest ever sexuality survey in 2003.

Referring to the loss of Anthony in 2013 for the Sydney Morning Herald, Dennis wrote:

> After death, one discovers there are many people who are kind, both friends and strangers; one also discovers there are people who are quite incapable of even the pretence of empathy [...]

> I sometimes wish we still lived in a society where one could wear mourning clothes, to as to signal to people that someone loved has just died. The hardest is to run into acquaintances who ask cheerfully, 'How are you?' Does one say, 'Fine,' or tell them? Usually I've done the latter, which certainly changes the conversation.[85]

'I was pulled into the international AIDS world for probably 20 years,' Dennis says now. 'That involved travelling a lot, which was actually very good in terms of our relationship. Sometimes Anthony and I travelled together, which was nice, and sometimes we didn't. But the lovely thing about going away when you're in a relationship is that you both get space, and then you have the excitement of coming back together again.'

Having lived through the full suite of Melbourne lockdowns, where the world of international travel felt like something fanciful Bessie and Fanny might find at the top of the Magic Faraway Tree, Dennis knows this excitement would have been lacking in recent years – as it clearly was for many others.

Even by early June 2020, a couple of months into a lockdown era that would splutter off and on until late 2021, the mediation service Relationships Australia reported that the number of people looking for advice on separating had far surpassed the previous year's figures.

The organisation's national executive officer Nick Tebbey said the surge seemed connected to the fact that 55 per cent of people in its study felt challenged by their living arrangements during lockdown:

> We are seeing that the kinds of calls and inquiries that our counsellors have received over the last few months are from people dealing with juggling working from home, looking after the kids and their home schooling [...] Basically, everything happening at home and them not being able to get out of the home.[86]

Culturally, that's been something of a revelation if not an outright revolution. Home – in whatever shape it takes – is supposed to be where the heart is. It's central to songs like 'Take Me Home, Country Roads', 'Our House', 'Sweet Home Alabama', 'Homeward Bound' – enduring hits that emphasise a yearning for home ... but always from a distance. Take away the freedom to come and go and the songs of the lockdown era are more likely to have titles like 'Stuck', 'My Own Prison' and 'Trapped In a Box'.

'I would have found it extraordinarily difficult to be in lockdown with a partner,' Dennis says. 'Relationships in my view need a lot of separate space. I've been very stuck watching some of my neighbours who are in couple relationships and who seem to have been quite happy to be locked together in a small apartment. I think I'd have found that stultifying and I think it would have made it very difficult for our relationship to survive.'

○○○

When Dorothy Porter died in 2008, the Fairfax Media wrote that:

> The Australian arts community is mourning the unexpected loss of one its true originals, the writer and poet Dorothy Porter, who died yesterday morning in Melbourne, aged 54, from complications from breast cancer.[87]

'To find myself in my late fifties, uncoupled, was a real shock to the system' says Andrea Goldsmith, Dorothy's long-term partner. 'At first, when Dot died, she was still walking into the room ahead of me, in a sense, because I was dealing with all the tributes and working on her unpublished books. There was no time, no private time to grieve.

'At the two-year mark, I fell apart. I'm the sort of person who, if I fall apart, nobody would know about it, but I found myself in serious life-threatening trouble. That's when I stopped doing all the tributes and tried to focus instead on living life alone.'

The connected issues for Andrea, as for others who find themselves in her situation, were not just being alone but being without her long-term partner. 'Grief takes many forms and I had to ask myself whether I really wanted to live,' Andrea says. 'I have a fear of other people's deaths but not my own.'

'I sought help, and part of coming out of that trough in which I found myself was working out what life would be like as a single person.'

In speaking with Andrea, it's clear that she didn't resolve to just put up with being single. She adapted to it and has found countless ways to make it work for her – a situation that underscores an obvious truth: while romantic relationships are often portrayed as the be-all and end-all in life, they all end, one way or another and life, while it lasts, goes on.

Andrea socialises with friends. She invites them to her house, cooks, entertains, and tells them to leave whenever she wants. She feels she has 'managed the single life reasonably well' – and she's not pining for anything else.

'One of my closest friends is the writer Drusilla Modjeska,' she says. 'She's been by herself for about as long as I have and before that always had a fella. We often say that we just don't want to have to put up with all the crap you have to put up with in a relationship.'

Part of that realisation for Andrea was about knowing what she wanted – another part came from seeing that what she wanted wasn't readily on offer.

'At the point at which I might have been open to somebody else, I looked around at men and women, wombats … No, not wombats, although I do like them … I saw all of these doddering old men and some very daggy women.

'I looked after Dot when she was sick and I did that without thinking. That was where I wanted to be, right with her at every appointment, between appointments, beside her in hospital. Looking around once she was gone, I thought, "I couldn't do that with somebody I'd just met and they have a stroke two years later". I'd want to hand them over to somebody else. So there hasn't been anyone since Dot and there won't be now.

'Having said that, if one day I was standing in my favourite cheese shop and someone came in, and they loved cheese, and they were single, and they were reasonably attractive, I'd buy cheese with them and go and eat it together.'

14
Getting better

Are things getting better in Australia? Yes, they are, according to the 2021 Mapping Social Cohesion Report by the Scanlon Institute, in which more than 70 per cent of respondents said they were optimistic about the country's future.[88] But given 60 per cent of people in that same survey agreed that racism was 'a very big' or 'fairly big' problem in Australia, it's worth remembering that the meaning of 'things' and 'getting better' depends on who and what you ask.

Still – 70 per cent is a lot. In 2022, the Survey Center on American Life found that only 47 per cent of Americans were 'very' or 'somewhat' optimistic about their country's future.[89] A 2021 survey by Britainthinks, meanwhile, found only 38 per cent of Brits were feeling positive about theirs – which doesn't surprise me, to be honest.[90]

On emigrating from Scotland to Australia in 2010, it was hard to avoid the sensation that people seemed generally happier here. The jetlag and confusion of being 17,000 kilometres from home couldn't cloud the fact that beautiful people were smiling beautifully – that they were essentially willing beauty into being.

'What can I get you?' a barista might ask.

'Um, a black coffee, please.'

'Beautiful. A long black?'

'Right, yeah. Um. I think so.'

'Beautiful. And what's your name?'

'Paul.'

'Col?'

'No, Paul. P-A-U-L. Like Paul Kelly.'

'Ah, right – Pauuuuul. Got it. Beautiful.'

From that moment, I saw and heard beauty everywhere I went. It perfumed my pessimism, dragged its happy feet through my dourness.

Still, that anyone, anywhere could be feeling sanguine at a time of pestilence, war and environmental endgame is curious. That said, it's probably better than despair.

In the Scanlon survey, there was an apparent correlation between the number of optimists and those responding positively to the statement 'Australia is a land of economic opportunity where in the long run, hard work brings a better life'. Which maybe suggests we're a positive and self-interested bunch, sandwiched somewhere between the UK's traditional belief in social support and the fevered, me-me-me American Dream.

And at least a bit of that optimism might be related to the sense that there's a growing tolerance of difference. Or better, the realisation that none of us should be labouring under the misapprehension that it's up to us to 'tolerate' or adjudicate the lives and loves of others. Or maybe that's my own misplaced optimism shining through.

The fact the Australian actor Rebel Wilson could effectively be 'outed' by *The Sydney Morning Herald* in 2022 is sobering. The move – bemoaning in a gossip column that Wilson ignored a request to comment on her romantic relationship with a woman – was as outdated, as writer Sisonke Msimang put it for *Guardian Australia* at the time, as the format in which the 'news' broke:

> Gossip columns first appeared in the 17th century, when print publications emerged. [...]
>
> Australia is a vastly different country now. [The Rebel Wilson] piece reflected the judgemental tone that has been the mainstay of gossip columns since they were first published in Victorian-era England.[91]

Not so much Back to the Future, in other words, but Back To the Past, and the more troubling question of: did we ever leave it?

Faith in the forward march of progress was surely severely tested by the treatment of trans people throughout the 2022 federal election campaign. Slurs and accusations abounded, many so nasty and ill-informed that it would make my hands wither to retype them here.

Add to that the dialling back of abortion rights in the US, plus any number of concurrently depressing realities in myriad walks of life, and it seems clear the cultural weathervane points many ways at once, signalling calm northerlies, stiff westerlies, incoming southerly busters.

But why might it be that trans people – including trans children – are facing such awful headwinds right now?

'It's something governments, particularly Liberal governments, have done successfully in the past,' Ellen van Neerven says. 'They target a marginalised group of people they feel they can pick on and who they see as the lowest denominator. It's a really shameful distraction technique, and obviously it backfired in the case of the 2022 election.'

Sport is an arena in which trans rights are debated and decided upon with little regard for the people – again, often children – most affected, knee-jerk rules and regulations imposed without, Ellen says, 'understanding the complicated nature' of the lives and issues in question.

'You know, to actually be a trans person and go through all of the transphobia and still actually compete in a sport is a miracle in itself,' they say.

'I feel like we're in a time as a society where there's a very strong emphasis on non-cis-male people's bodies and what they can and can't do with them. If you look at the *Roe v. Wade* stuff in the States, I just can't help thinking these things are tied together somehow, where some people are really impeding other people's rights to do what they want with their bodies. I don't understand it, or why it's happening right now, but it's real fearmongering.'

The notion that 'things' are improving, in this sense at least, seems ludicrous. 'Yeah, it's strange,' Ellen says. 'It goes against what LGBTQIA+ people of my generation were told, that it gets better. You reach a point where you're like, "Well, I don't I think so, actually. I'm just a political football that's going to be kicked around". Maybe we should interrogate some of our political systems and structures to find out why certain rights can just be stripped away and whether the people governing us are a broad representation of society.'

○○○

Having given it as much thought as I can while writing this book, I feel fairly confident about the following statements. Australia is prudish. Australia is broad-minded and permissive. Australia is racist. Australia is aspirationally – and sometimes demonstrably – anti-racist. Australia is sluggish on matters of sexuality and gender. Australia is forward-thinking (and occasionally world-leading) on matters of sexuality and gender. Australia should be ashamed to leave the house. Australia should remember, and be happy about, all the many things it gets right.

And if that's nationally, my feeling is that it's similar for most individuals. We're rarely all things all at once, or even *one thing* at once – more often, we're some things at some point, equivocating at the equator rather than pushing from the poles. The main – and constant – variable seems to be how we see ourselves in relation to those around us at any given moment.

'The idea of being able to be 100 per cent declarative of any position is really difficult for me now,' Christos Tsiolkas says.

With his 2019 novel *Damascus*, he virtually wrote the book on doubt, given its focus on the Bible's 'doubting' Thomas.

'*Damascus* is one of the books I'm proudest of,' he says. 'There's the question of faith and the question of doubt, and the question of how you hold those things together.'

As we're chatting, he touches on something that's been on my mind quite a bit of late, a type of sacrilege I'm generally scared to mention. As welcome as it is that certain shibboleths are crumbling – particularly around sex, gender and the granting of power and privilege – it sometimes feels like new certitudes have taken their place, alongside an insistence, implied or otherwise, that this – this! – is the new truth, heretics be damned.

This bothers me because I'm resistant to orthodoxy in whatever form it takes, even when I agree broadly with the script. I don't just think good ideas *should* be open to stress-testing – I believe they *have to be* tested regularly and rigorously, like a kindergarten smoke alarm. If you *know* your ideas are the right ones, free of grit and incapable of causing harm, then good on you – in some ways, I envy your conviction.

'There's something of religious fervour in some of the politics of the moment that I find disquieting,' Christos says. 'I don't think it's an accident that "woke" is a term that comes from evangelical awakening, and of course that's because of the cultural dominance of the US. For me, feminism is the sun and queer politics is the moon and those politics have been so instrumental and integral to my life, but I do feel the current espousing of those politics is quite puritanical.'

I tell Christos about a podcast I heard once about the performance artist Vito Acconci, whose 1972 work *Seedbed* involved him lying under gallery floorboards in the US and jerking off while whispering lewd comments to the people walking above. I've never been able to find that podcast again, despite searching for it, but the point I took away was that the work was designed to scandalise conservatives, which it did, whereas these days it would surely repel conservatives and progressives alike.

Although we'll likely never know. Nobody, I assume, is in a rush to restage *Seedbed* in a major gallery – and, in my view, that's probably for the best.

Christos in turn talks about *Piss Christ*, the 1987 photograph by the US artist Andres Serrano in which a plasticated, crucified Jesus is pictured inside a vat of Serrano's urine.

'That work comes out of HIV and AIDS,' Christos says. 'It asks the question: where is Christ? If we're saying he's in the piss and the shit and the blood, then that's actually a radical Christian understanding'

In the '80s, *Piss Christ* was derided as deviant left-wing art, prompting a congressional debate on US public arts funding. Religious opposition to the work peaked in 2011 when French Catholic fundamentalists attacked it with hammers.

And yet, here's what Serrano himself said in 2012: 'At the time I made *Piss Christ*, I wasn't trying to get anything across. In hindsight, I'd say *Piss Christ* is a reflection of my work, not only as an artist, but as a Christian.'[92]

Christos says 'the people who want to ban that work these days are from both the left and the right. I don't know how we got here. There's almost a sense that, in a deeply secular time, we're creating religions out of ideology.'

When it comes to art as an authentic reflection of life, this is problematic. 'It's the fear that worries me,' Christos says. 'There's a real cowardice now among artists and writers, and I count myself among that. We all understand the historic reasons for taking a break and thinking "maybe it isn't my place to speak", but I was in a workshop yesterday where someone was arguing about Picasso.

'And yes, of course I can condemn the misogyny of his behaviour but one of the most important memories of my life is being in the Reina Sofía in Madrid and standing in front of [Picasso's famous 1937 painting] *Guernica*. I just think it's one of the greatest anti-war statements ever. It's stunning. When you contemplate the scale of the painting and what it is … So I'm like, "Fuck off. Actually, fuck off, I'm not giving up *Guernica* for you". That to me is censorship.

'I will raise my hand and proclaim history,' he says. 'It terrifies me what the right can do, what conservatives can do, because when they come in they can annihilate. But on the left, this type of thing is not new either – they were doing it in the 1930s, saying, "We're going to censor this art because it's difficult or dangerous or incorrect". I'm not saying these politics aren't complicated – just that some of the aspects we're seeing again now aren't new.'

○ ○ ○

Christos and I were dancing carefully around something that, I think, plays out most obviously on Twitter and other social media sites, where debate has gone from a long-rally model to a rapid serve-and-volley game or, more commonly, a series of attempted aces down the line. People say and think nonsense all the time, which goes just as much for the highly literate and sensitive as it does for bigots and trolls. But there are differences between thinking, saying and believing.

My dad used to tell me this story about his time in the navy. As punishment for losing a training exercise, he and his colleagues had to take off their uniforms and run naked back and forth for twenty minutes through a dense thicket of stinging nettle bushes, after which the drill sergeant ordered them into a line and asked if anyone had anything to say. Nothing. Just welts and torn skin.

Eventually, one man put his hand up and asked sheepishly if they could be punished for thinking.

'Of course not, you bloody idiot,' the drill sergeant barked.

'Oh good,' the private said. 'Cos I think you're a fucking bastard.'

Many of us – the cannier ones – know the basic etiquette of keeping our unconsidered views far from social media and company email servers. Many of us – the guileless, uninformed, clumsy and mean – don't. Watching concerted takedowns of anyone espousing obvious bigotry or other types of undeniably gross misconduct, it's hard not to think, 'Serves you right, mate'. But there are also those times when someone's hasty proclamation or badly played bon mot drops just the wrong side of the net, whether through a genuine mistake or an imperfectly worded punchline that, for all we know, would make us laugh if we had the benefit of interpersonal context, intonation and facial expressions. Watching people being pummelled in those instances, it can be hard not to think, 'There but for the grace of god ...'

'Social media has really changed the landscape,' Lee Kofman says.

I tell Lee that, for me, it sometimes feels as if the heavy indignation of certain people purporting to be on the left, when added to that of the far right, is squeezing all the oxygen from the room.

'That's not surprising,' Lee says. 'Having grown up in the Soviet Union, I really have a good nose for that kind of thing. I've always been on the left, before coming to Australia and since being here, but I'm increasingly finding it much easier to talk to people on the moderate right. I don't agree with them, and I'm not scared to tell them what I think, but the difference is they're more likely to listen to me. When you talk to people who are very adamantly on the left, they often just shut you up – there's no argument, no debate, you're just shut down.'

○○○

As always, though, there are reasons to be cheerful.

'I'm excited about the future,' Rob McDonald says. 'We've had this weird thing for a long time in terms of political power where it's one group, the white cis male who nine times out of ten is either heterosexual or at least heterosexual-facing, which is bizarre. When you think about the diversity of our community, why would you have this one group making calls for everyone? It actually doesn't make sense.'

Changing this, he thinks, will be multigenerational, but the work has already begun. 'I mean, I'm Gen X and we were just like, "This is fucked, we're bailing",' he says. 'But the Millennials are breaking this down now, and I'm obviously a parent of Gen Z kids. I just love that we have a generation growing up who are like, "Why is it like this? It shouldn't be this way". To which I'm like, "Yeah, you're right".'

I'm reminded of something Filip Vukašin said, about how he hopes homosexuality, and by extension other forms of sexuality and gender expression, 'needs to lose its gloss, to be just like your eye-colour'. Would Rob like to see that too?

'I'd like it if nothing was assumed before a child wished to disclose their gender and sexual preference,' he says. 'That they could tell you, whenever they wanted, they're asexual or pansexual, bisexual or poly. I think we've got to move away from the default being heterosexual. I understand hetero reflects the majority but it's only a majority because Western Christian culture has forced it to be the default. There are so many ways of being and flavours and fluidity alongside that idea of a rigid heteronormative nuclear family.'

○ ○ ○

Rob's (and Filip's) views echo Dennis Atman's prediction more than 50 years ago of a society embracing 'a fluid and diverse sexuality that does not need categories'.[93]

Dennis nods when I mention this in the context of progress towards greater freedoms around sexuality and gender. 'I would say, for all the things people still find to complain about, that, at least in the rich Western world, it's a lot easier and better now than it was,' he says. 'If we're talking about life in Australia, all one has to do is think about the careers of a number of very prominent people who are openly homosexual – the classic case being [Labor Senator] Penny Wong.

'Penny is widely respected and seen by many people as a potential prime minister, and at the same time is known to be both lesbian and Asian, both of which would have disqualified her for a parliamentary seat 40 years ago.

'I don't think one should ever underestimate the progress. I know there are people who come up against things and they get very upset, and I've seen someone being booed at a conference for basically saying what I've just said about things getting better. I think that's very sad because I think one doesn't have to say everybody has equally bene-fitted to point out the extent to which social norms have changed.'

Would he like to take a punt at how the next 40 years might pan out? Are we heading for the swinging 2060s or something altogether different?

'I'm struck by the fact that, for many young people, there's a much more complicated way in which they play with identity politics, where they want to both adopt and resist labels,' he says.

'You know, the gravity of the climate crisis is such that in 40 years my garden in [inner-city] Clifton Hill will probably be beach-frontage.

'The one thing I've learned as a political scientist is that predictions are almost always wrong. Maybe one or two will be right, and if you're very clever, they're the ones you remind people about.

'But I do think the language we're using now is not the language we'll be using in ten years' time. And I hope some of the willingness to attack anyone who doesn't seem to follow the prescribed rules of identity politics will decline.

'There's a mean-spiritedness at the moment towards anyone who doesn't follow the right terms and accepted behaviour, a tendency to think of those people as enemies. I hope that will pass, but the truth is I won't be around to see it and for all I know things might get much worse.'

○○○

'For what it's worth, I think the next generation at least feel like they have more options,' Rochelle Siemienowicz says. 'They don't necessarily have to choose them, and they'll make their own mistakes, but at least they know they exist. My son's straight but he went out to a gay nightclub last week with his pansexual friend and said the music was great for dancing. Meanwhile, a girl he knows is going out with two boys at the same time and she's not being shamed for that.

'That generation is already defining their relationships and their sexuality with more flexibility and creativity than we ever did, with more acceptance of ethical nonmonogamy, kink and asexual romantic connections. Whether that's the case outside of urban centres, I'm not sure, but I do feel a sense of hopefulness.'

More stories, real and imagined, will help, she thinks, as well as much more honest talking. 'In recent years, I've found that when I talk to people about my polyamorous family, the responses are overwhelmingly positive and curious, rather than harshly judgemental. This is especially the case from older women in long-term relationships.

They have a real sense of "there must be more' and "perhaps there are other ways of doing things', even if they're sceptical about their own ability to manage jealousy and the needs of more lovers.

'There's no utopia in sight, but it feels like there's a bit more acceptance.'

○ ○ ○

My sons regularly surprise me with their literacy in identity politics – they're so far ahead of where I was, where *anyone* I knew was, at their age. As I was filling in an online form some years ago, my younger son, who was seven at the time, said it was old-fashioned that the gender options were only male or female. He didn't say it to score points, he wasn't grandstanding – he was simply pointing out what for him was obvious.

I'm of an age and type of dodgy social wiring where, when we're watching a show like *Schitt's Creek* as a family and the characters David and Patrick are kissing, I feel myself tensing up. I think it's because I expect my kids to ask what's going on or laugh or think it's somehow weird that two men are smooching. They don't flinch. In one scene, in which David alludes to his sexuality by telling his best friend Stevie that he drinks red wine, but also white wine, as well as sampling 'the occasional rosé', my 11-year-old asked if that meant he was pansexual. And then just nodded casually when I told him it did.

As I was driving them both to Jess's place a few weeks ago, we got into an impromptu discussion about pronouns after one son mentioned that a couple of the kids in his friendship group are non-binary. We talked about those children's preferred pronouns, and then my son said I'd never asked him his.

'Oh, sorry, mate, what are they?' I asked.

'I'm happy with "it",' he said.

'It?' I said, laughing, slapping the steering wheel. 'Is that really what you want? *It*? HAHAHAHAHAHAHA.'

'Why are you laughing?' he asked.

I looked at him, back at the road. 'You're … You're not serious, are you?'

'What if I was?' he said. 'Do you think it would make me feel good that you're laughing at me?'

'Well, no,' I said. 'Probably not.'

Honestly, I don't know if he was being serious or winding me up and we haven't returned to the topic yet, but I appreciate the point he was making. What if he *does* want his pronoun to be It? What if that was him/it coming out to me and my reaction was to laugh about … it. And what if, alongside the pronoun, he/it declared his/its sexuality was something that, simply because I'd not heard of it before, made me slap the steering wheel again?

The best antidote to those fears, or similar ones, might be to set the words to one side for a second and focus on the person saying them.

'The reality is that the lexicon we have inherited to make sense of "sexuality", as many people in the western world understand it, was invented by psychiatrists in the early 1900s,' Arlie Alizzi says. 'These terms are functional. They organise us into social groups, but I would argue that they shouldn't be adhered to as if they contain an essential truth about us.'

○○○

A fair whack of political anxiety seems to stem from a paranoia that diversity is transmissible and that all of us, unless we guard against it, are its potential victims. Suppressing, denying, persecuting and poking fun are all ways of mitigating the terror that the 'unusually' masculine, feminine or non-binary vampire is going to sink its fangs into our necks. Ronald Reagan's famous 1980s joke that a hippy was someone 'who looks like Tarzan, walks like Jane and smells like Cheetah' worked only because his audience would have assumed a hippy (and everyone else unless otherwise specified) was a man, and then found it laughable to think of that man having a 'womanish' gait and long hair.

From Julia Gillard being described by a Liberal senator in 2007 as 'deliberately barren'[94] to the Australian comedian Rhys Nicholson having homophobic abuse hurled at him on a packed Melbourne train in 2018,[95] it's clear that the impulse to ward off anything other than straight conservative demonstrations of a life properly lived is still very much among us. But surely that can change.

If, in Patrick Mullins's words, Australia is a country where we're 'constantly knocking on the bathroom door to find out what you're doing inside', then maybe we can learn to walk past without knocking anything or anyone, instead giving people time and space to be whoever and whatever they want.

'For me, it's about giving language to things that have always existed,' Chris Cheers says. 'When people find the words that help them understand themselves, that's a useful thing. But I also believe the more we act against the dominant binary male and female, and the idea of heterosexual as being "right", that starts to dismantle the constructs of gender and sexuality.'

How does he see this working in practice?

'My hope is that, with more labels reflecting our diversity, we'll start to lose the idea of sexuality and gender as something that *is* our identity,' he says. 'They just won't be as important to how we view ourselves.'

Gender, he thinks, is key. 'If we stop using gender to evaluate who you should be in a relationship with, to determine who we should give the power to and who we should listen to, we're going to enter this space where someone's sexuality isn't important either, because sexuality is often based on the gender of the partner you're attracted to.'

Of course, there are biological differences between people assigned male at birth and those assigned female, he says, but those M and F terms are, let's face it, pretty basic.

'In some sense, we're let down by our minds, because they have to categorise and try to process the world around them,' Chris says. '"Male" and "female" are something we've created and put on our bodies. Sexuality is something we've created and put onto our understanding of sex. I think it's useful to question those categories.

'Without them, what we're left with is human beings and the fact that we're all animals. When you think about all the diversity among the group we call male, all the diversity among the group we call female, all the diversity among the group we call non-binary, I think we can start to connect to the idea that these categories probably aren't as useful as we think they are. What do they mean if the group within them is so diverse?'

○ ○ ○

In recent years, I've had a recurring thought that sometimes gives me vertigo. It's linked to the rails on which I thought life ran, a 'common-sense' track that didn't need to be scrutinised too intently precisely because it was common sense.

That it was advantageous for me to leave school at 14, say, because it meant I could more quickly gain a trade, the common-sense move for a working-class boy to make. From there, it was common sense, or at least very likely, that I'd meet someone – a cis female pepper shaker to go with my cis male salt – after which we'd take out a mortgage that cost about four times our yearly wage, and probably have kids. I'd pursue the same line of work for many years, most likely in the same city, saving money whenever I could, going on yearly package holidays and getting maudlin at the work Christmas night out. We'd pay off our house, retire, wear the bottoms of our trousers rolled, die.

The rupture is obvious. I've had a mortgage before (in the UK, pre-GFC) but don't foresee having the capital or heart for another. As with a job for life, a decent pension, or even retirement as it was previously understood, homeownership has become more of a wish-list item for many people than a common-sense reality. And rather than living in the same city, I've been jumping from place to place since I was twenty-two.

The recurring thought I've been having isn't so much about that rupture but the fact those rails that seemed to emerge from time immemorial only went back a generation. My grandparents lived through one world war, their parents through two. All were born before penicillin was invented and before the National Health Service was founded in the UK. Relationship and gender norms were probably as infused with Victorian and Edwardian double-standards as they are now, but otherwise the rails their lives ran on were as different to my parents' tracks as they were to those of their own grandparents, who lived before domestic electrification and the federation of Australia.

The vertigo I feel is related to my kids and what I'm supposed to tell them life 'should' be like. Through homeschooling, the Black Summer bushfires and the unsustainability of capitalism as we know it, I've had to force myself to encourage them to do anything other than live in the moment because I can't imagine their future, or anyone's, looking anything like the present or recent past. Naïvely, I'd love it if they could look back on these pandemic years as a discreet shitstorm that happened in the past, at weather events of unprecedented frequency and ferocity as the sort of things that got really bad for a while before settling down, at the 2020s – as they've played out so far in Australia and elsewhere – as a weird blip rather than the first of many bends on a rapidly descending helter-skelter for humanity, a slippery slope, if you like, but one that merits the alarm.

Given the collective energy that's urgently needed to confront those issues, I won't be wasting any of mine wringing my hands over my children's, or anyone else's children's, relationship choices, gender expression or sexuality.

My greatest hope for them, for all of us, really, whether single, hetero, poly, swinger, straight, vanilla, gay, kinky, lesbian, trans, sex worker, non-binary, dom, sub, male, female, gender-neutral, agender, pangender, genderqueer, intersex, queer platonic, asexual, unsexual, hyper-sexual, celibate, a combo of these, none of these or something else entirely, is that we find more ways to unashamedly console ourselves and each other, that we pull together with genuine and meaningful community-mindedness, or at least not stand in the way of those who are trying their best.

Notes

1   'The Census is compulsory, every response matters: Media Release'.
    Australian Bureau of Statistics. 06.09.21. www.abs.gov.au/media-
    centre/media-releases/census-compulsory-every-response-matters
2   'Sample 2021 Census Household Form'. Australian Bureau of Statistics.
    www.abs.gov.au
3   'Topics not included in the 2021 Census'. Australian Bureau of Statistics.
    16.11.2020. www.abs.gov.au/statistics/
    research/2021-census-topics-and-data-release-plan#topics-not-
    included-in-the-2021-census
4   *Ghostbusters*. Columbia Pictures. 1984.
5   'Bernardi resigns after bestiality comment'. ABC News. 19.08.2012.
    www.abc.net.au/news/2012-09-19/
    controversy-over-cory-bernardi-bestiality-comments/4269604
6   *The Sex Lives of Australians: A History*. Frank Bongiorno. Black Inc.,
    2015, p. 165.
7   *The Trials of Portnoy*. Patrick Mullins. Scribe Publications, 2020, p. 173.
8   'The Crimson Thread Speech'. Foundation 1901. Grand Banquet at
    Melbourne. https://foundation1901.org.au/the-crimson-thread-speech/
9   Peter Cowan interviewed by Stuart Reid for the Battye Library
    collection [sound recording]. Trove. https://nla.gov.au/nla.obj-
    217140734/listen
10 'Writing Sex Should Be (Un)Easy: A Guest Post by Paul Dalgarno'.
    04.11.2020. LeeKofman.com
11 *Poly*. Paul Dalgarno. Ventura Press, 2020. pp. 227–228.
12 *The Pillars*. Peter Polites. Hachette. 2019, p. 58.
13 *Son of Sin*. Omar Sakr. Affirm Press, 2022, pp. 36–37.
14 'He's not my father, he's my husband'. Ruth Dawkins. The Guardian.
    21.05.2011. www.theguardian.com/lifeandstyle/2011/may/21/
    older-husband-young-child
15 'My husband is 70. I'm 35. I've become a Dear Abby for others in
    relationships with large age gaps'. Ruth Dawkins. The Washington Post.
    09.11.2018. www.washingtonpost.com/lifestyle/2018/11/09/
    my-husband-is-im-ive-become-dear-abby-others-relationships-with-
    large-age-gaps/

16   'How Much Does Age Matter in a Relationship?' Theresa E. DiDonato Ph.D. Psychology Today. 29.05.2021. www.psychologytoday.com/au/blog/meet-catch-and-keep/202104/how-much-does-age-matter-in -relationship

17   'Mind the gap – does age difference in relationships matter?' A/Prof. Gery Karantzas. SEED: Centre for Social and Early Emotional Development. Deakin University. www.deakin.edu.au/seed/our-impact/mind-the-gap-does-age-difference-in-relationships-matter

18   'Australian Social Trends'. Australian Bureau of Statistics. 2013. www.abs.gov.au/statistics/people/people-and-communities/australian-social-trends

19   'Why couples with big age gaps are happier, despite the social disapproval'. The ABC. 20 April 2018. www.abc.net.au/news/2018-04-20/couple-with-a-larger-age-gap-happier

20   A Superior Spectre. Angela Meyer. Ventura Press. 2018, p. 44.

21   Transcript: Ezra Klein Interviews Dan Savage. The New York Times. 10 January 2023. www.nytimes.com/2023/01/10/podcasts/ezra-klein-show-transcript-dan-savage.html

22   Money for Something. Mia Walsch. Echo Publishing, 2020, p. 80.

23   'How Coronogamy (Coronavirus-Induced Monogamy) Has Changed My Sex Life'. Jinghua Qian. 25.6.20. www.mtv.com.au/news/8rk1hz/how-coronogamy-coronavirus-induced-monogamy-has-changed-my-sex-life

24   'I Am Not The Role Model You're Looking For'. Holden Sheppard. 01.04.2021. https://holdensheppard.wordpress.com/2021/04/01/i-am-not-the-role-model-youre-looking-for/

25   'Julie Peters on 50 years at the ABC and 30 years blazing a trail as a trans woman'. ABC News. 04.03.2022. www.abc.net.au/news/backstory/2022-03-04/julie-peters-50-years-abc-tv-30-years-trailblazing-trans-woman/100879806

26   A feminist post-transsexual autoethnography on challenging normative gender coercion. Julie Peters. 2016. https://dro.deakin.edu.au/view/DU:30086469

27   'Brotherboys And Sistergirls: We Need To Decolonise Our Attitude Towards Gender In This Country'. Junkee. 20.06.2020. junkee.com/brotherboy-sistergirl-decolonise-gender/262222

28   'Men's self-reliance linked to risk of self-harm'. Pursuit. University of Melbourne. 13.03.2007. https://findanexpert.unimelb.edu.au/news/2468-men%E2%80%99s-self-reliance-linked-to-risk-of-self-harm

29   Modern Marriage. Filip Vukašin. Affirm Press, 2021, p. 35.

30   'Benjamin Law: Coming Out (Again)'. Queerstories podcast. Maeve Marsden. 08.03.2017 https://maevemarsden.com/queerstories/episodes/benjamin-law-coming-out-again/

31   'Polyamory and the mirror on the wall'. Paul Dalgarno. Archer
      Magazine. 15.10.2020. https://archermagazine.com.au/2020/10/
      polyamorory-the-mirror-on-the-wall/
32   'Sex Discrimination'. humanrights.gov.au
33   'Gay conversion therapy banned in Victoria after marathon debate'. The
      Age. 04.02.2021.www.theage.com.au/politics/victoria/gay-conversion-
      therapy-banned-in-victoria-after-marathon-debate-20210204-p56zls.
      html
34   'Free2Be... Yet?: The Second National Study of Australian High School
      Students Who Identify as Gender and Sexuality Diverse'. Jacqueline
      Ullman. 2021. https://doi.org/10.26183/3pxm-2t07
35   'Bisexuality: The Invisible Letter "B"'. Misty Gedlinske. TedxOshkoh.
      23.01.2019 https://youtu.be/Oa6AnOCQD50
36   *Polysecure: Attachment, Trauma and Consensual Nonmonogamy.*
      Jessica Fern, 2020, Thornapple Press, p. 154.
37   *Sex at Dawn: The Prehistoric Origins of Modern Sexuality.* Christopher
      Ryan and Cacilda Jethá. Harper Perennial, 2010, p. 98.
38   *Nanette.* Hannah Gadsby. 2018. Netflix.
39   *Homosexual: Oppression and Liberation.* Dennis Altman. University of
      Queensland Press, 1971.
40   *The End of the Homosexual.* Dennis Altman. University of Queensland
      Press, 2013, p. 209.
41   'Becoming with and together: Indigenous transgender and transcultural
      practices'. Arlie Alizzi. 01.06.2017. www.artlink.com.au/articles/4604/
      becomingE28091with-and-together-indigenous-transgender
42   'Meet Omar Sakr: Australia's queer Arab poet'. ABC News. 04.06.2017.
      www.abc.net.au/news/2017-06-04/omar-sakr-australias-queer-arab
      -poet/8558940
43   *These Wild Houses.* Omar Sakr. 2017. Cordite Books.
44   'Ace up my sleeve: Coming out as asexual'. Gabrielle Ryan. *Archer.*
      08.11.2018. archermagazine.com.au/2018/11/
      ace-up-my-sleeve-coming-out-as-asexual
45   *More Than Two, A Practical Guide to Ethical Polyamory.* Franklin Veaux
      and Eve Rickert. Thorntree Press, 2018, pp. 138–39.
46   *Wreck-It Ralph.* Walt Disney Studios Motion Pictures. 2012.
47   'Fixing the refrigerator: How to deal with jealousy'. More Than Two
      Blog. Franklin Veaux. www.morethantwo.com/jealousypractice.html
48   '"Do you get jealous?": the six questions I always get asked about being
      polyamorous'. Paul Dalgarno. Guardian Australia. 02.09.2020. www.
      theguardian.com/lifeandstyle/2020/sep/02/do-you-get-jealous-the-six-
      questions-i-always-get-asked-about-being-polyamorous
49   *The Dangerous Bride.* Lee Kofman. University of Melbourne Press, 2014,
      p. 292.

50 'Is Polyamory a Form of Sexual Orientation?' Elisabeth A. Sheff. 04.10.2016. Psychology Today. www.morethantwo.com/ jealousypractice.html

51 'Building a Household'. Simon Copland. *Queerstories: Reflections on lives well lived from some of Australia's finest LGBTQIA+ writers*. ed. Maeve Marsden. Hachette, 2018, p. 174.

52 pp. 183–84

53 'Purity culture is dehumanising – it's consent that should be at the centre of sex education'. Chanel Contos. Guardian Australia. 01.02.2023. www.theguardian.com/commentisfree/2023/feb/01/purity-culture-is -dehumanising-its-consent-that-should-be-at-thecentre-of-sex -education

54 'Health Check: how often do people have sex?'. The Conversation. 25.02.2019 https://theconversation.com/ health-check-how-often-do-people-have-sex-108423

55 'A multinational population survey of intravaginal ejaculation latency time'. Marcel D Waldinger, Paul Quinn, Maria Dilleen, Rajiv Mundayat, Dave H Schweitzer, Mitradev Boolell. 2005. National Library of Medicine. https://pubmed.ncbi.nlm.nih.gov/16422843/

56 'Read Me: Angela Chen's Ace Challenges Us All to Reframe How We Talk About Sex'. them. 15.09.2020. www.them.us/story/ read-me-angela-chen-ace-interview

57 'Ace up my sleeve: Coming out as asexual'. Gabrielle Ryan. 08.11.2018. Archer Magazine. https://archermagazine.com.au/2018/11/ ace-up-my-sleeve-coming-out-as-asexual/

58 *Fallen*. Rochelle Siemienowicz, Affirm Press, 2015, p. 54.

59 *The Dangerous Bride*. Lee Kofman. University of Melbourne Press, 2014, p. 21.

60 *Eye of A Rook*. Josephine Taylor. Fremantle Press, 2021, p. 7.

61 *The Philosophical Baby: What Children's Minds Tell Us About Truth, Love, and the Meaning of Life*. Alison Gopnik. Farrer, Straus and Giroux, 2009.

62 *Flash Gordon*. Columbia–EMI-Warner Distributors. 1980.

63 *Dumb and Dumber*. New Line Cinema. 1994.

64 *Bridget Jones's Diary*. Universal Pictures. 2001.

65 'I've written a novel about polyamory – not a manifesto'. Paul Dalgarno. The Herald. 15.11.2020. www.heraldscotland.com/news/18860288. paul-dalgarno-ive-written-novel-polyamory---not-manifesto/

66 'Ain't Love Grand': The Erasure of Bisexuality in Buffy the Vampire Slayer'. Kat Muscat. Kill Your Darlings. 04.10.2014. www.killyourdarlings.com.au/article/aint-love-grand-the-erasure- ofbisexuality-in-buffy-the-vampire-slayer/

67   'Seeing Ourselves: Reflections on Diversity in Australian TV drama'. Screen Australia. 2016. www.screenaustralia.gov.au/fact-finders/ reports-and-key-issues/reports-and-discussion-papers/ seeing-ourselves

68   'Does Polyamory Fall Under the LGBT+ Umbrella?'. Kim Barrett. 25.01.2020. Medium. https://medium.com/polyamory-today/ polyamory-and-the-lgbt-community-3a8a52debbc3

69   *The Naked Ape: A Zoologist's Study of the Human Animal*. Desmond Morris. Random House, 2010, p. 86.

70   'Household and families: Census'. Australian Bureau of Statistics. 28.06.2022. www.abs.gov.au/statistics/people/people-andcommunities/ household-and-families-census/latest-release

71   'Polyamory – Not Healthy For Children'. Dr Karen Ruskin. 28.10.2013. www.drkarenruskin.com/polyamory-not-healthy-for-children

72   'Children in Polyamorous Families: A First Empirical Look'. Elisabeth Sheff. 2013. www.researchgate.net/publication/279456619_Children_ in_Polyamorous_Families_A_First_Empirical_Look

73   'Second Reading Speech: Marriage Amendment (Definition and Religious Freedoms) Bill 2017'. 04/12/2017. Prime Minister Malcolm Turnbull.PM Transcripts. https://pmtranscripts.pmc.gov.au/release/ transcript-41362

74   'Attorney-General George Brandis' powerful same-sex marriage speech, in full'. The Sydney Morning Herald. 28.11.2017. www.smh.com.au/ politics/federal/attorneygeneral-george-brandis-powerful -samesexmarriage-speech-in-full-20171128-gzu669.html

75   '500 years of European colonialism, in one animated map'. Zack Beauchamp. Vox. 16.01.2015. www.vox.com/2014/5/8/5691954/ colonialism-collapse-gif-imperialism

76   'Factbox: Belgium's colonial rule in Congo and what happened next'. Charlotte Campenhout and Bate Felix. Reuters. 09.06.2022. www.reuters.com/world/africa/belgiums-colonial-rule-congo-what -happened-next-2022-06-08

77   'Earth system impacts of the European arrival and Great Dying in the Americas after 1492'. Alexander Koch, Chris Brierley, Mark M. Maslin, Simon L. Lewis. Quaternary Science Reviews. 01.03.19. pp. 13–36. www.sciencedirect.com/science/article/pii/S0277379118307261

78   'Hiding the bodies: the myth of the humane colonisation of Aboriginal Australia'. John Harris. Aboriginal History. Vol. 27 (2003). ANU Press. p. 81.

79   'Tony Abbott welcomes axing of Safe Schools anti-bullying program in NSW'. The Guardian. 15.04.2017. www.theguardian.com/australia- news/2017/apr/16/nsw-to-drop-safe-schools-anti-bullyingprogram -when-federal-funds-expire?

80   'The harmful 'Safe Schools' Program – Our children deserve better!'. Labour DLP. https://dlp.org.au/the-harmful-safe-schools-program-our -children-deserve-better/
81   'Safe Schools Victoria'. Vic.gov.au. https://www.vic.gov.au/safe-schools
82   *Unrequited Love: Diary of an Accidental Activist*. Denis Altman. Monash University Publishing, 2019, pp. 102–103.
83   *All About Yves*. Yves Rees. Allen & Unwin, 2021, p. 282.
84   *'Dating two people at once: why I'm polyamorous and proud'*. Simon Copland. The Guardian. 26.05.2015. www.theguardian.com/ society/2015/may/26/dating-two-people-at-once-why-im -polyamorous-and-proud
85   'Life after Anthony'. Dennis Altman. The Sydney Morning Herald. 9.03.2013. www.smh.com.au/lifestyle/life-after-anthony-20130304- 2ff8z.html
86   'Post-lockdown divorce: jump in number of Australian couples seeking help'. The Guardian. 18.06.2020. www.theguardian.com/australia- news/2020/jun/18/post-lockdown-divorce-jump-innumber-of -australian-couples-seeking-help
87   'Dorothy Porter dies'. The Sydney Morning Herald. 11.12.2008. www. smh.com.au/entertainment/dorothy-porter-dies-20081211-gdt63x.htmll
88   'Mapping Social Cohesion 2021'. Scanlon Foundation Research Institute. https://scanloninstitute.org.au/mapping-social-cohesion-2021/
89   'Americans Are More Optimistic Than You Think'. American Survey Center. 14.03.2022 https://www.americansurveycenter.org/ americans-are-more-optimistic-than-you-think/
90   'Most Britons pessimistic about their immediate future, survey finds'. Financial Times. 31.12.2021. https://www.ft.com/ content/08d13d12-2a96-4020-88c9-eb5fb666559a
91   'The Rebel Wilson uproar shows that gossip columns belong in a bygone era'. The Guardian. 18.06.2022. www.theguardian.com/ commentisfree/2022/jun/18/the-rebel-wilson-uproar-shows-that- gossip-columns-belong-in-a-bygone-era
92   'Artist bears his cross in career retrospective'. The Sydney Morning Herald. 02.10.2012. www.smh.com.au/entertainment/art-anddesign/ artist-bears-his-cross-in-career-retrospective-20121001-26v8e.html
93   *The End of the Homosexual*. Dennis Altman. University of Queensland Press. 2013. p. 209.
94   'Heffernan's "deliberately barren" the most sexist remark of 2007'. The Sydney Morning Herald. 13.11.2007. www.smh.com.au/national/ heffernans-deliberately-barren-the-most-sexist-remark-of-2007- 20071113-gdrl0m.html

95   'Comedian Rhys Nicholson endures homophobic rant on Melbourne train. The Sydney Morning Herald'. 20.03.2018. www.smh.com.au/ entertainment/comedy/comedian-rhys-nicholson-endures-homophobic-rant-on-melbourne-train-20180320-p4z5az.html

Acknowledgements

My heartfelt thanks to:

Terri-ann White for commissioning this book and for what, by any measure, is an amazing track record of publishing work by writers, and on topics, that enrich our sense of what books and ideas can do.

Martin Shaw, my agent, who came up with the idea that led to this book being written. He also came up with the title. Thank/blame him.

Emily Stewart for her astute editing and insightful notes in the margins.

To all of the interviewees who, through their generosity, time, body of work and openness to discussion, make this book what it is.

To Kate, as always, for putting up with me, and also for reading an early draft and being one of a kind.

To my kids because, four books in, I still can't imagine doing acknowledgements without acknowledging that they mean more to me than anything.

This book was written on the land of the Wurundjeri people, in a council area recently renamed Merri-bek, with thanks.

About Upswell

Upswell Publishing was established in 2021 by Terri-ann White as a not-for-profit press. A perceived gap in the market for distinctive literary works in fiction, poetry and narrative non-fiction was the motivation. In her years as a bookseller, writer and then publisher, Terri-ann has maintained a watch on literary books and the way they insinuate themselves into a cultural space and are then located within our literary and cultural inheritance. She is interested in making books to last: books with the potential to still be noticed, and noted, after decades and thus be ripe to influence new literary histories.

About this typeface

Book designer Becky Chilcott chose
Foundry Origin not only as a strong,
carefully considered, and dependable
typeface, but also to honour her late
friend and mentor, type designer Freda
Sack, who oversaw the project. Designed
by Freda's long-standing colleague,
Stuart de Rozario, much like Upswell
Publishing, Foundry Origin was created
out of the desire to say something new.